Nurturing the Beloved Community

Nurturing the Beloved Community

The Art of Building and Sustaining Life Together

Jonathan Herbert

First published in 2026 by Canterbury Press

Editorial office
3rd Floor, Invicta House
110 Golden Lane
London EC1Y 0TG, UK
www.canterburypress.co.uk

Canterbury Press is an imprint of Hymns Ancient & Modern Ltd
(a registered charity)

HYMNS Ancient & Modern

Hymns Ancient & Modern® is a registered trademark of
Hymns Ancient & Modern Ltd
13A Hellesdon Park Road, Norwich,
Norfolk NR6 5DR, UK

British Library Cataloguing in Publication data

A catalogue record for this book is available
from the British Library

ISBN: 978-1-78622-716-4

EU GPSR Authorized Representative
LOGOS EUROPE, 9 rue Nicolas Poussin, 17000, LA ROCHELLE, France
E-mail: Contact@logoseurope.eu

Typeset by Regent Typesetting

Contents

Acknowledgements

I'm grateful for the inspiration of the communities I've lived in and visited. The Simon Community, the L'Arche community, the Catholic Worker Houses and particularly Pilsdon Community, which continues to shape me. I continue to appreciate the generosity of Hilfield Friary Community in giving me such a rich life, copious material to think about and the time to write. Thanks in particular to Brother John for his gentle encouragement.

The Sisters of the Sacred Heart at Llannerchwen continue to teach me the importance of curating silence. Sue Langdon with her wise accompaniment and rich contemplative life allows me to feel held more fully in the love of God.

To all my Gypsy and Traveller friends, thanks for drawing me into the riches and challenges of your community life, with thanks to Ivy Manning and Betty Smith Billington who've taught me so much.

My involvement with Christian Climate Action and their combination of risky actions alongside pilgrimage, vigil and prayer, teaches me how community can be formed around prophetic witness. Thanks to three of my closest companions on this journey: Hilary Bond, Ruth Jarman and Sue Parfitt.

Thanks to Sarah Cotterell and Martin Newell for comments and advice, Beth for technical assistance and, last, to David Shervington for patient and wise editorial support.

Introduction

It's raining hard as people slowly arrive for a weekend entitled 'Mandalas and Franciscan Spirituality' at Hilfield Friary on a November afternoon. Visitors join us for tea and toast either side of the ten-metre-long communal dining table filling the refectory. Some have been many times before, others have come for the first time and tuck into homemade bread and jam and tea from big steel pots, and feel the welcome of this 100-year-old community. There's something about this time that seems to express the warmth and inclusion of our community: you could be sitting next to a four-year-old or a venerable bearded Brother in a habit, someone who is homeless, an overseas student, a person struggling with their mental health or an exuberant extrovert, and somehow our common table holds all in community. I look around and am filled with gratitude for the community I'm gifted with living in.

After supper, our weekend begins with some joint reflections on gratitude and then participants are invited to create their own circular mandala of thankfulness. There's a big table of pens, paint, paper, plates to draw round, buttons, gemstones and coloured sticks, and people begin to form their mandalas. I just can't get mine right and keep adding more and more to it and it just feels wrong. As the session ends, we gather to look at each other's work and I know instantly what's wrong with mine: there's no gaps or space, it's crammed full with too much stuff. Everyone else has worked this out and produced some beautiful work.

The following day we create a Lamentation Mandala on the red-brown tiled floor, which fills the back of the chapel. Silently, we draw a circumference with a string attached to a stick in the centre and someone on the outside moving around while shaking out bright white builder's lime until the circle is closed. More lime is used to draw four quadrants, then black charcoal is dotted on the thick chalky lines. Then grey ash is sprinkled into each quarter and four words – anger, fear, grief and emptiness – are drawn into it and stand out starkly, rather like letters on a misted window. A thick stick is placed next to anger, a cold piece of flint for fear, a shrivelled leaf for grief and an empty bowl in the final space. People are then invited in their own time to walk into a quadrant, hold the symbol and speak a couple of short sentences as we listen in silence. It's raw, people share deeply. My first instinct is that I want to get out and have a nice cup of tea or, better still, a stiff drink, but I know I need to stay with my difficult feelings rather than distract myself. We stay in the space silently or go for solitary walks, then after an hour gather to debrief.

That afternoon we gather a large bunch of four-metre bamboo canes, barrow loads of apples and leaves and struggle uphill to a north-facing grassy slope. Tony happens to have his chainsaw, so cuts a dozen mat-like rings from a large nearby log and, surrounded by meadowland, hedgerow and the woods, we construct a ten-metre-wide mandala. Spokes of bamboo reach outwards, apples at the centre, dots of wood spaced out symmetrically, layers of burnt bracken and a thick circumference of autumn leaves. We finish just as the sun fades beneath the trees. I say, 'Now would be the time to have a drone', but Tony suggests a photo from a large step ladder, which he climbs and captures the mandala set on the hill with the woods and autumn sky behind it. And yes, the people who helped make it huddled together, dwarfed behind it, beaming out joy.

Constructing the mandalas seems to contain most of the themes of this book. How do we build and nurture community and what are the virtues that keep it alive? I'll look at some of the forces pulling society apart and then further chapters examine what over 30 years of living in residential communities has taught me about the essential values that create community wherever we are.

We sited our big mandala on a hill with an expansive view, and vision is the first of these essential requirements, for vision creates inspiration, gives direction focus and can strengthen our resolve in difficult times. As the book of Proverbs says, 'where there is no vision, the people perish' (Prov. 29.18, KJV). The vision of St Francis has inspired countless people for eight centuries and continues to underpin our life at Hilfield.

Marking out the edges of the mandala represents the need for good and healthy boundaries in our common life; boundaries keep us safe and help define the vision. Awareness of our limitations and the limits of the natural world can give a community sustainability and prevent it unravelling. The Rule of Benedict has much wisdom when it comes to establishing healthy patterns of living with others.

My experience of failing to produce a decent-looking mandala while working on my own symbolized the need for members of a community to embrace humility. There's such a temptation in a world that teaches self-reliance to try and do things on your own, compete with others and cram as much as possible into life. I'm slowly learning my need of others and seeing how humility makes room for others. The spirituality of Charles de Foucauld and the Little Sisters and Brothers of Jesus has much to teach us about humility.

Entering the Mandala of Lamentation and speaking our truths about grief, fear, anger and emptiness wasn't easy, but built trust in our little group. Finding ways to build and maintain trust allows a community to grow and be resilient in the face of many challenges. In a world where trust in institutions is constantly being eroded, building communities with strong healthy relationships has never been more important. Carmelite spirituality offers a rich resource for thinking about trust.

Those attending the workshop all came with a variety of needs and were welcomed into a community that seeks to look outwards. Responding to the practical and spiritual needs of others gives communities purpose and prevents them becoming self-centred. The Catholic Worker Movement and the writing of Dorothy Day epitomize this.

Collecting the apples and leaves and pushing them uphill before assembling the mandala was hard physical work but bound us together as a community. Doing common tasks reminds us of our need for each other. Working outdoors also reminds us we are part of a much bigger earth community. The Cistercian tradition speaks into this.

Standing on the steps looking at our mandala, the wider creation surrounding it and the group gathered together filled me with joy and gratitude. Gratitude is at the heart of maintaining community life, affirming people and our mutual endeavours. Times of celebration are there to remind us to constantly give thanks for the giftedness of life and the goodness of the Giver. Ignatian spirituality offers some good tools for embedding gratitude in our individual and community lives.

What follows is my attempt to make sense of what has bound together the communities I've lived in over the last 30 years, but is also an offering to all who seek to build community wherever they find themselves – whether a community association, a group of neighbours, a local church or a residential community. As society continues to fragment and communities are attacked by the merciless forces of corporate greed, we need to have deep roots and strong networks of support in order to resist these pressures. In the 1960s, Martin Luther King often spoke of the need for the 'Beloved Community' to sustain the Civil Rights Movement and drew strongly on the resources of Scripture in the Christian tradition. Sixty years later there's an even greater need to nurture beloved communities.

1

Community

I'm standing in the middle of the A40 at Gypsy Corner, Acton, in west London. In front of me are three lanes of cars and vans quickly backing up into a major morning rush hour traffic jam. Behind me is a row of some 12 protestors, sitting cross-legged and calm on the cold tarmac. They clutch three red, white and blue plastic banners with the simple message 'Insulate Britain', and are all clad in matching orange high-visibility waistcoats. It's getting noisy, car horns are pressed permanently down and volleys of abuse are coming our way. Some people sit in their cars grim faced, holding in the stress, others let it all out, swearing repeatedly, 'Get an effing job', 'Some of us have to work you stupid bastards ...' or the slightly more nuanced, 'We support your ideas but this isn't the way to bring about change.' I've been tasked with de-escalation, so rather than sitting in the road I'm walking round trying to keep things calm. My best line seems to be, 'The police will be here very soon; they'll arrest people then you'll soon be on your way.' I'm doing my best but today it's chaos. I see a man in the free-flowing traffic on the other side of the carriageway pull his white van onto the central reservation and come sprinting towards our seated roadblock. I try to get between him and my companions, but he pushes me out of the way, grabs a banner and rips it out of the hands of those below him. He scrunches it up and goes for the next one, throws that away and the action somehow dissipates his anger and he's off back to his van telling us and everyone what he thinks of us. From the opposite carriageway a carton of steaming coffee, thrown from a van window spills out in front of the grounded activists. Things feel like they're getting out of control as I turn back to try and speak with those standing outside their stationary vehicles. Also engaging, interviewing and egging on drivers are journalists from LBC Radio, *Good Morning Britain* and the *Daily Mail*. There's a cheer as someone sprays green paint over the line of seated protestors and then relief for me as the police arrive. Immediately, the drivers' rage and impatience is turned on the police for not acting quickly enough. I see a thickset man rushing towards us snarling with fury and I try to intercept him but as soon as he sees the police, he turns away, saying to me, 'If the police weren't here, I'd have killed someone.'

I turn to try and assist a policeman with de-escalation, but he rounds on me furiously asking me to step back and let him handle the public. I'm slightly taken aback, always thinking of myself as quite a good mediator, then his logic hits me. Of course, I'm the cause of all this, provoking the public, and now I crazily think I can help things calm down. Chastened, I sit down next to my friends and wait to be arrested. I feel a bit left out as the only one not covered in green paint, as the cameraman from *Good Morning Britain* pans along the stained row and begins interviewing Mark, a gentle clergyman who wipes his inky glasses and explains why he's there. Almost immediately I have to get up out of my lane to allow an ambulance to get through, then I can sit, relax and wait. I'm soon handcuffed and led away to the police transport, which today bizarrely is a double-decker bus.

Sitting on the top of the bus, a wave of fear washes over me. It's nothing to do with the confrontations of the morning but rather it feels like I've had a taste of the future. It's a glimpse of what's coming our way in the next 20 years or so and it's going to be pure chaos. What's been played out this morning could be what our country looks like in the future as the climate crisis begins to take hold and what we know as civil society begins to break down, amid food shortages and economic and political stresses.

What was happening at Gypsy Corner involved four protagonists: the delayed drivers, the police, the media and the protestors, and all have something to teach us about the growing fault lines in our society and the breakdown of community across the world.

The drivers

The drivers delayed by our actions had a variety of reactions, ranging from resignation to yet another delay on our overcrowded roads, to low levels of anger and to explosive rage. It's the group venting their anger that most scared me. What rattled me was the huge outpouring of rage and frustration that seemed to represent a very dystopian future. It felt to me that the people bellowing out their frustrations at us could be among the first to be attracted to simple clear messages coming from the far right and a 'strong leader', rather like those who stormed the Capitol in support of Donald Trump in Washington in January 2021.

As a well-educated 60-year-old white man, I've seldom experienced such aggression as I met on 'Insulate Britain' roadblocks, save from dealing with the occasional angry or drunk person I'd had to exclude from the community I lived in. Reflecting on the experience of this outpouring of visceral rage with a couple of Traveller friends, I was able to get a glimpse into their world and their fears for the future. Unlike the experience of most Travellers, we were being targeted for good reason and had chosen to put ourselves in a position to be abused. We'd delayed people going to work, going to hospital appointments, visiting the sick, getting children to school. We clearly deserved the ire we were attracting, we were prepared for it, knew we were provoking it to draw attention to a bigger issue. I knew all this, but the hatred of the mob whipped up by the media against 'Insult Britain' and its 'ecomob' showed how quickly a group can be demonized and be a convenient scapegoat for society's ills.

History clearly shows that when economies begin to fail, people will begin to target groups to blame. It happened most clearly in Nazi Germany with the targeting of Jews, the Roma and others who were blamed for society's ills. In Ancient Rome it was groups like the Christians. In medieval Spain it was the Jews and the Muslims expelled by Ferdinand and Isabella in 1492. That same year Columbus' voyage to the Americas began the othering of native peoples that was used to justify the subsequent colonial enterprise. I fear that as the climate crisis inevitably leads to more and more forced migration, climate refugees will become more heavily and explicitly targeted by the extreme right, as will Britain's 500-year-old scapegoat – Gypsies and Travellers.

As civil society further unravels, the temptation to vote in a strong leader and party with an agenda of blame that allows people to dump their growing discontent on an easily recognizable group with a strong law and order agenda will be widely supported. It's already happening in the UK with the 2022 Police, Crime, Sentencing and Courts Act, with its draconian legislation limiting peaceful protest and, in particular, its use of Part 4, which criminalizes trespass.

This part of the Act is specifically aimed at unauthorized encampments of Gypsies and Travellers and gives the police powers to fine, impound vehicles (people's homes) and imprison Travellers for simply pursuing a nomadic way of life or just being homeless on the roadside. Billy Welch, a Romany Gypsy, who organizes the Appleby Horse Fair, told me a story that illustrates how far we as a country are lurching towards authoritarianism and how under threat his community feels. Twenty years ago he was travelling in Germany when he met some German Roma and Sinti people, who told him how in the 1930s the Nazis had begun their persecution of his people by first confiscating the Roma's waggons and horses. Then they began fining them and finally started to imprison them. He said to his new German friends, 'That could never happen in the UK.' However, 20 years on the impounding of vehicles, fines and imprisonment are happening to nomadic people here. It's popular too, and seen as a vote winner.

It was ironic being arrested at Gypsy Corner, but salutary for me to gain a tiny bit of insight into the kind of abuse that Travellers who park on the roadside tell me they experience every day. Horns honking, stones thrown at caravans and threats to burn them out. I've seen 'Die Gypsy' graffitied in red onto the side of a trailer and heard of empty petrol cans being left outside trailers.

Other drivers were more quietly furious with our actions, being delayed from getting to work and getting on with business as usual. They experienced the delay as yet another factor compounding the stress of daily living. We live in a fast-moving world, where communication is rapid and transport systems, when they are working well, move people around at speed. The much slower, more considered movement and communication systems of our ancestors have been replaced by instant communication and the ability to travel swiftly. We think nothing of flying across continents, while in 1954 the England cricket team took five weeks to travel by boat to play in the Ashes series. Jim, a Traveller friend who lives off-grid and travels by horse and waggon, goes a maximum of 15 miles per day. 'It's crazy the speed people are travelling at these days, it's no wonder we have a mental health epidemic,' he told me. The drivers, temporarily becalmed by our actions, all with deadlines and places to go, are caught up in what the Buddhist philosopher and activist Joanna Macy called the 'Industrial Growth Society'.

> Like Alice on the chess board of the mad queen, we must run ever faster to stay in the same place. What is in store for our children's children? What will be left for those who come after? Too busy running to think about that, we try to close our minds to nightmare scenarios of want and wars in a contaminated and wasted world.[1]

Macy here captures well the trap so many of us are caught up in, seemingly to have to work faster and longer to keep up with ever rising rent, mortgages, bills and so many other costs. We live what Thoreau called 'lives of quiet desperation'.

The temptation is to retreat into the bubble of our individual needs and those of our immediate families and hang on for survival rather than challenge a system that only seems to be working for the richest 10 per cent. This way people cling on, but it puts people under constant stress and mitigates against a more humane society where people have time for one another and can pursue the common good.

In 2018, 74 per cent of the population of the UK admitted to feeling 'overwhelmed or unable to cope' at some point in the previous year and, alarmingly, 32 per cent of adults experienced suicidal feelings as a result of stress.[2]

When you add on the stress of thinking about climate change and its catastrophic consequences it's easy to give in to the temptation to just get on with things, work a bit harder in the deluded hope that things will get better for your nearest and dearest.

So many of the motorists were the sole occupants of their vehicles, which highlights the growing individualism of our society, its attendant loneliness and the erosion of community support. It's now estimated that 31 per cent of the UK population live in single households.[3] This has led to an epidemic of loneliness and isolation that in turn leads to poorer mental and physical health.

When we act as individuals, we are prey to numerous addictions. The more we are encouraged to think and act for ourselves, the more we lose the bonds of community that are there to sustain us and the lonelier and more frustrated we become.

For those on the road who told me they were sympathetic with our cause but not our methods and let us know how much we were damaging the cause of moving to more sustainable living, there was no easy response. If I'd had the time, I would have sat down with them, tried to listen to their concerns and then told of my 30 years of trying petitions, lobbying politicians, marches, vegetarianism, installing insulation and low-carbon technology, not flying and trying to live simply – and how nothing had changed. The change we need can only come through decisive and rapid action and needs to happen very soon. In 2021 Sir David King, former Chief Scientific Advisor to the Government, speaking at the Melbourne National Climate Emergency summit said, 'What we do over the next three to four years, I believe is going to determine the future of humanity. We are in a very desperate situation.'[4] Understandably, facing up to the huge challenges of the clear and present danger of the climate crisis seems just too much to contemplate for people ground down by the stresses of day-to-day survival.

If the drivers felt under pressure, how much more are those serving in our police forces under stress? And that stress is only likely to increase as the climate crisis, with its attendant food shortages, storm and flood damage, inexorably harms the economy and destabilizes society.

The police

Having been arrested a number of times for peaceful non-violent protest, I've been able to do some very informal anecdotal research on the incredible pressures the Metropolitan Police, the City of London Police force and Essex Police are under. After arrest, I'm usually accompanied by an officer for two or three hours before being booked into a cell at a police station. This gives time for some good one-to-one conversation. I always try to build a relationship with my arresting officer and begin by apologizing for the disruption I have caused to them individually, but I will also briefly explain my fears for the future of the planet and society. I say I don't take the breaking of the law lightly and explain how in the past I've been grateful for the protection the police have offered when I've had to call them in an emergency. Then I try to listen to them and learn something of the daily challenges they face. Time and again they tell me that rather than protecting people and preventing and investigating crime they are acting as social workers. Many speak of how much of their time is taken up dealing with the lack of resources given to mental health services, supporting people who are homeless and the victims of addiction, rather than being out on the streets protecting people.

As I listen to these police men and women who are all dedicated public servants, telling me of the trauma of dealing with knife crime, suicides and the epidemic in mental illness, the breakdown in society, of which they are on the front line, becomes clearer and clearer to me.

Perhaps where the breakdown in society is most starkly illustrated is in our prison system. Over 90,000 people are locked up and with the chronic underfunding of the prison system many are regularly in their cells for 23 hours a day with little chance for exercise, meeting other prisoners or the chance to participate in education or work. Low pay and low morale mean that recruitment and retention of prison officers is difficult; on average new prison officers stay for only 12 months. This constant changeover of staff in the prison makes for high levels of stress and a lack of stability in each institution. When I visit a wing where there are experienced officers who know how to build relationships with prisoners, there is a feeling of calm and security, but too often the pervading feeling is of insecurity and poor communication.

The stressed policeman at Gypsy Corner, infuriated by my attempts to offer mediation between him and a member of the public, seems a good symbol of those tasked with dealing with the stresses of a society facing multiple forces that are destroying the human spirit.

One of these forces is undoubtedly the media.

The media

At Gypsy Corner there were reporters from the *Daily Mail*, *Good Morning Britain*, Sky News and LBC Radio, plus, no doubt, several hundred people sharing pictures on social media. The reporters were hostile to Insulate Britain and I could see them doing interviews through car windows and overheard one or two questions. 'How does it make you feel being deliberately stopped from getting to work?' 'What do you think of these people disrupting your lives?' It felt like the press were seeking to provoke anger and inflame people's frustrations. Taunts to us, like 'Get a job!', 'You stinking crusties!' and 'You're causing more pollution by blocking traffic you idiots!', all could be traced back to things said on the airwaves or in tabloid headlines. The genius of Insulate Britain was that through its disruptive tactics, it got extensive coverage. Admittedly, the majority of the story would be about the disruption caused by the 'selfish ecomob', but when protestors were allowed a voice, the message about the need for insulation did get through: how insulation could raise people out of fuel poverty, save lives, create jobs, and is the quickest and cheapest way to lower carbon emissions. Brave spokespeople for the organization were savaged on talk shows and in other media, but persisted with trying to put over the one simple demand to insulate leaky homes.

I found it difficult to see good and honourable people vilified by the media for campaigning against the existential threat to the survival of the human race, let alone numerous other species threatened by climate change. The media have been complicit in the silence around our need to dramatically and speedily re-orientate how our economy works if we are to have any chance of a sustainable future in the coming years. Since the 1970s, oil companies have known of the existential threat of the climate crisis caused by burning fossil fuels but, with the assistance of the media, played down the seriousness of the situation. For years it was perfectly respectable to be a climate denier in spite of the overwhelming scientific evidence: both sides of the 'debate' had to be aired on channels like the BBC. Think tanks like the Global Warming Policy Foundation, sounding respectable but quoting dubious science supported by few academics, were funded by oil companies to deliberately obfuscate and play down the need for the radical economic and societal change needed to slow down the climate emergency.

It's sobering to think that in the last 30 years since governments have clearly received and understood the science of climate change and pledged to take action, carbon dioxide emissions have increased by 50 per cent, according to the Institute for European Environmental Policy (29 April 2020).[5]

The mainstream media have, with a few exceptions, consistently promoted the status quo and the economic growth at all costs agenda. In the UK, the ownership of newspapers is controlled by a handful of billionaires. Some of whom, like Rupert Murdoch, are active climate deniers.

By doing something as disruptive and confrontational as blocking roads, Insulate Britain finally got the attention of the media. I'd been on huge marches highlighting the climate crisis attracting tens of thousands, which rarely get a mention on the news. In June 2018 I was part of a huge lobby of Parliament on the climate crisis organized by a coalition of NGOs that involved over 10,000 people. So many were there, that lobbyists stretched in a line nearly a mile long, along the Thames through Parliament Gardens, across Lambeth Bridge and all along the South Bank in front of St Thomas' Hospital. There was no media coverage save a brief mention in *The Guardian* the next day. Yet Insulate Britain brought out the media in force, as there was a clear, simple story to tell and a group to easily identify and demonize. There was a clear conflict between the selfish lawless 'ecomob' and ordinary members of the public facing severe disruption. The tabloids loved us as there were endless dramatic pictures of stupid protestors being dragged away by members of the public having to take the law into their own hands and numerous stories of the hurt and anger caused to delayed drivers.

Too often the media, like most of the population, seems to be in denial of the dangers we face in spite of the overwhelming scientific evidence. Every year the Intergovernmental Panel on Climate Change (IPCC), a neutral body made up of the world's finest scientists, issues dire warnings. Yet, given the enormity of what they are predicting, it gets little coverage. Even after temperatures reached over 40°C in parts of the UK in July 2022, and over 40 fires broke out spontaneously in Greater London, there was little sustained reporting on increasing temperatures. On 19 July 2022, with the temperature reaching 40°C, the London Fire Brigade had its busiest day since the Blitz in 1940.[6] The same day, freed from the restraints of working for the BBC, one of its most respected and mild-mannered former journalists, Andrew Marr, issued a blistering critique of government inaction on his LBC radio show:

> I for one have had enough of being told by pallid, shadowy old businessmen and lazy ignorant hacks and sleazy lobbyists, who aren't real scientists, any of them, that the science is wrong ... it needs to be called out and flushed out right now ... And if you don't believe me, go outside and have a brisk walk.[7]

Sadly, Andrew Marr seems to be something of an exception among mainstream journalists in being prepared to aggressively voice his concerns. This has led to the activists being forced into increasingly desperate publicity-seeking actions.

The morning after my first Insulate Britain roadblock, everyone in the house we were staying in had returned from the cells, and we were having breakfast together when someone came in with a sheaf of the morning papers, which he spread over the table. There we were, pictured all over them with derogatory headlines. As we read down some articles there was mention towards the end not only of obstruction and disruption but also of the need to insulate the UK's leaky housing stock.

On the following Friday night, Brian even managed to get onto the satirical BBC News show *Have I Got News for You* with a picture of a protestor who'd glued his face to the tarmac with his inhaler for asthma just inches away from his outstretched hand. It raised a lot of laughs, but what wasn't mentioned was the despair Brian had been in over the Government's announcement that same day, that it would be providing part-funding for 5,000 air source heat pumps. 'What about the other 24 million homes dependent on gas boilers?' he asked, 'Gluing my face to the ground was an act of desperation!'

He had a vision for the future far beyond that of the Government but here he was being ridiculed for seeing the bigger picture, written off as a selfish agitator and self-publicist. My experience of meeting, working with and indeed being one of the 'ecomob' felt quite different.

The protestors

At the roadblocks I attended, I sat next to a former policeman, a former member of the parachute regiment, a retired solicitor, a retired teacher, a management consultant, a bricklayer, an 80-year-old priest, a youth worker, a musician, a small business owner and several young people fearful for the future. None really fitted the description of 'environmental terrorists' that they have been labelled with. My experience and that of so many others who've chosen to go down the route of civil disobedience and non-violent direct action is that as well as pushing me well out of my 'comfort zone', the greatest benefit has been the friendships I've made with some wonderfully committed and compassionate people. It's meeting with fellow protestors and activists that gives me hope for the future.

Of the hundreds of people I've met on actions, I've yet to meet anyone who falls into the thoughtless, selfish, irresponsible idiot stereotype of the tabloids. Everyone involved in groups like Extinction Rebellion, Insulate Britain, Just Stop Oil has to undergo non-violence training or they're not eligible to be part of a team. People come with a variety of motivations. Those who've studied for degrees in environmental science or marine biology, and in the face of the alarming facts, feel compelled to do something; young people who don't see any future for themselves in a world of climate-change-induced economic and political chaos; elders who fear for the future of their grandchildren; people of faith who feel compelled to defend God's creation; lovers of nature who are so grieved by the destruction of trees, creatures and whole ecosystems that they feel impelled to act; those who've heard the stories of refugees from places like Sudan and Syria where the climate crisis was a big cause of conflicts that have forced them to leave home.

Always the night before an action, protestors will 'check in' and introduce themselves to each other, often articulating their motivations for risking being part of tomorrow's activity. It's moving to hear a little of people's stories and see the respect and love with which they are listened to, and it's here in the formation of this temporary community that I find hope.

Martin Luther King spoke about the importance of forming 'the Beloved Community' in the struggle for civil rights in 1960s USA. King understood that without the beloved community and its practical, emotional and spiritual support, activists would soon burn out. Groups like Extinction Rebellion and Christian Climate Action, who exist on the front line of action to highlight the climate emergency, are highly skilled at building networks of support. People are able to meet regularly to support and encourage each other through 'live' or online meet-ups. Extinction Rebellion speaks of the need for 'regeneration' of activists, so fallow periods are built in between programmes of action. Numerous opportunities for training and supporting each other are offered. One of my favourite workshop titles is 'Composting Our Grief', which explores how fear and despair can be transformed into positive action. There are listening circles, affinity groups, arrest support, prison support and numerous other ways to ensure people don't become isolated but feel part of a wider mutually supportive community.

As we move towards a world where there are likely to be growing shortages, we will need resilient and compassionate communities to survive the multiple onslaughts. In his paper

'Deep Adaptation', climate scientist and sociologist Jem Bendell graphically describes the coming breakdown he foresees:

> When we contemplate this possibility [of societal collapse], it can seem abstract ... But when I say starvation, destruction, migration, disease and war, I mean in your own life. With the power down, soon you wouldn't have water coming out of your tap. You will depend on your neighbours for food and some warmth. You will become malnourished. You won't know whether to stay or go. You will fear being violently killed before starving to death.[8]

These extremities may not be happening in the UK yet but lest we become complacent such climate-breakdown-related circumstances are already forcing people to flee their homes in many parts of the world. As Warsan Shire so graphically tells in her poem 'Home':

> You only leave home
> When home won't let you stay[9]

Home is breaking down for so many people in the world, whether literally, by flooding, famine or climate-change-induced conflict, or spiritually, through the breakdown in community caused by neo-liberalism's culture of greed and individualism.

As I become more convinced in the science that tells us that we're heading towards some irreversible tipping points, I'm thinking that the time has come to transfer my limited energy away from civil disobedience and towards thinking about how to build resilient communities that can mitigate some of the intense suffering and privations that could soon be part of daily life. This has been the work of Jem Bendall and others who are part of the 'Deep Adaptation' movement that is growing across the world. As a Christian I'm fascinated by the language Jem Bendell uses, much of which aligns with my tradition. When he talks about relinquishment, restoration, reconciliation, he's using terms full of deep resonance for Christians. This, in turn, has led me to want to explore what there is in the Christian tradition that can be of use to help sustain societies that are falling apart. The question I want to begin to answer is: what is there in the long history of Christian spirituality that can be of use in creating a more resilient society, one which will mitigate against the huge forces of destruction that are upon us? Writing with great prescience in 1981, Alasdair MacIntyre reflected how moral life survived the Dark Ages due to the development of monastic life:

> This time, however, the barbarians aren't waiting beyond the frontiers; they have already been governing us for some time. And it is our lack of consciousness of this that is part of our predicament. We are waiting not for a Godot, but for another – doubtless very different – St Benedict.[10]

Hope coming out of adversity

What gives me hope is the kind of compassion and solidarity that I experienced alongside activists from Christian Climate Action, Just Stop Oil and Insulate Britain, and also my 30-odd years living in intentional communities. I vividly remember, as a child, my Irish grandmother over from Belfast sitting at the kitchen table reminiscing with another older woman about the hardships of the war, the rationing, the bombs, the fear, but the thing that stood out for me was her joy in remembering what had also been a time of intense community solidarity and the building of friendships. Her English friend also enthused about her wartime experience. As a child I was a bit bemused by this paradox of good times coming out of bad. Later on, working among the homeless, I met many an ex-serviceman struggling to cope outside the community of belonging provided by the army, who'd also repeat similar stories of the intense sense of kinship and trust built up on the battlefield and in times of danger.

This longing for a sense of corporate solidarity, belonging and common purpose is what drew me into living in community and keeps me here. In these dangerous times, the ways of self-sufficiency, competition, individual achievement, and striving for financial security will lead to yet more violence, in the face of what's to come. Instead, we need to find new ways of living, which may in fact be embracing some very old ways. Living in community has meant the surrender of a lot of autonomy, such as being able to do what I want exactly when I want it, independence, building a career, money, the choices it gives and a well-planned social life; but it has given me so much more. Learning to depend on others and have them depend on me, and in turn realize I'm part of a much bigger community of other living beings on this earth, has allowed me to loosen the shackles of fear and insecurity and walk more lightly on the earth and really value the people I have been given.

At Pilsdon Community, where we offered hospitality and accommodation to homeless men and woman, there was a Glaswegian wayfarer named Joe, who'd visit just two or three times a year. We always ended up giving him a few more days than the standard three nights, because he was such a creator of community. Well into his 70s, he'd turn up with all his belongings packed tightly into an old army rucksack. He'd been a strong man in his day, and had packed quite a punch in his wilder drinking days, but now like Jacob after his wrestling with the angel, limped badly on a damaged hip. He could no longer manage any heavy work but took up residence by the kitchen sink, singing away as the heavy communal pans crashed into the soapy water under his thorough scrutiny. I always felt a bit guilty passing him yet another one, but he always looked up, smiled and replied in his thick Glaswegian accent, 'Nae Bother!' Once finished he'd sit on the bench outside rolling a cigarette and sharing tobacco and conversation with whoever took up the offer to sit alongside his genial presence. The last time I saw him was when I gave him a lift to the motorway junction near Taunton. I pulled into a layby and jumped out of the car, struggling to lift his heavy bag out of the boot as he limped up beside me. Suddenly I fully felt his physical fragility. 'Will you be all right, Joe?' I asked and, grinning, he replied, 'Someone's been looking after me all these years, so I think I'll be all right today. Nae Bother!'

The day I left Joe I had a feeling of fear for him, much like the fear I have for my own children and grandchildren in the turbulent times that are coming. What I'm continually learning, though, is that, like Joe, embracing a simpler life, as well as being necessary for all to accept if we are to survive as a people, also brings me more joy than anything else. Likewise, though sometimes a big struggle, living in community and building networks of friendships is what brings security and deep contentment. As Dorothy Day, the founder of the Catholic Worker Movement, said, 'We have all known the long loneliness and what we need is love, and love comes with community.'[11] How we build community is what I wish now to explore.

Notes

1 Joanna Macy, 2011, *Coming Back to Life*, Gabriola Island, Canada: New Society Publishers, p. 16.

2 Mental Health Foundation, 2018, '74% of UK overwhelmed or unable to cope at some point', *Mental Health Foundation*, 14 May, https://www.mentalhealth.org.uk/about-us/news/survey-stressed-nation-UK-overwhelmed-unable-to-cope, accessed 19.01.2026.

3 Office for National Statistics, 2022, 'Families and households in the UK: 2021', *Office for National Statistics*, 9 March, https://www.ons.gov.uk/peoplepopulationandcommunity/birthsdeathsandmarriages/families/bulletins/familiesandhouseholds/2021, accessed 19.01.2026.

4 David King in Benjamin Silvester, 2021, 'Forget 2050, experts say it's 2030 or bust for net zero emissions', *The Citizen*, 12 February, https://www.thecitizen.org.au/articles/forget-2050-experts-say-its-2030-or-bust-for-net-zero-emissions, accessed 19.01.2026.

5 Institute for European Environmental Policy, 2020, 'More than half of all CO2 emissions since 1751 emitted in the last 30 years', *Institute for European Environmental Policy*, 29 April, https://ieep.eu/news/more-than-half-of-all-co2-emissions-since-1751-emitted-in-the-last-30-years/, accessed 16.03.2026.

6 London Fire Brigade, 2022, 'London Fire Brigade declares major incident as second day of heatwave sparks several significant fires across the capital', *London Fire Brigade*, 19 July, https://www.london-fire.gov.uk/news/2022-news/july/london-fire-brigade-declares-major-incident-as-second-day-of-heatwave-sparks-several-significant-fires-across-the-capital/, accessed 19.01.2026.

7 LBC, 2022, 'Andrew Marr's furious response to those dismissing the climate crisis LBC', *YouTube*, 19 July, https://www.youtube.com/watch?v=-dCCuLrisNo, accessed 21.01.2026.

8 Jem Bendell, 2018, 'Deep Adaptation: A Map for Navigating Climate Tragedy', IFLAS Occasional Paper 2, https://insight.cumbria.ac.uk/id/eprint/4166/1/Bendell_DeepAdaptation.pdf, p. 11.

9 Warsan Shire, 2016, 'Home' in *Poems that Make Grown Women Cry*, London: Simon and Schuster, p. 268.

10 Alasdair MacIntyre, 1981, *After Virtue*, London: Duckworth, p. 263.

11 Dorothy Day, 2009, *The Long Loneliness*, New York: HarperCollins, p. 243.

2

Vision

It's a cold clear frosty February morning as Rupert and I load the chainsaws and ropes into the back of the rusty but reliable Toyota pick-up and set out for Dorchester. Rupert is an arboriculturist staying with us at Pilsdon, and I'm secretly elated, as, with Rupert's back hurting, I'm going to get to climb and fell the tree today. It's always fun to work with Rupert because he has a wicked sense of humour and a great love and respect for nature. He went to sea to get away from drugs, working on deep-sea fishing trawlers only to end up drinking heavily. Back ashore he qualified as a tree surgeon and took up the equally dangerous pursuit of tree climbing. His exuberant love of nature is stirring something in me. What's keeping him sober is having outdoor work to do. We arrive at the job, which is to cut down a dead 60-year-old silver birch to make room for the householder's new and bigger car. 'Ah! *Betula pendula*! Named after the drooping branches. The silver bark in the younger trees is great for lighting fires. One of my favourite trees,' Rupert enthuses. 'Sorry you won't get to climb today, we can fell it in one go.'

I start the saw and swiftly cut a felling wedge out of it, but we are shocked to see sap pouring out of it. It's as if the tree is bleeding. I know then the tree is still alive, but that we've mortally wounded it. Stunned, I ask Rupert what we should do. As a deep ecologist he's furious, but says that the tree will never recover and is now unsafe, so we'll have to fell it. I cut from behind the wedge and it topples over with a mighty crash, and I feel like a murderer. I've killed a perfectly healthy tree and all for the sake of making room for a bigger car. It seems a parable of the destructive tendency of unregulated global capitalism and market forces. Destroy something that nurtures you to promote economic growth. The tree had made way for the upgraded, more expensive car; something living had been destroyed to make way for a machine. I know I've been complicit in what feels like a murder.

Later that evening, I'm in a tutorial class on eco-spirituality with Professor Mary Grey and tell the story of the tree felling and how it has affected me, and at the end of the group she reads from 'The Dream of the Rood', an early Anglo Saxon poem told from the point of view of the tree that Christ is crucified on. I feel like I've crucified the tree and been caught up in the ongoing destruction of the natural world.

That evening, something begins to shift in me, and I know I have to do more to protect the earth I had begun to love so intensely. I begin to be inspired by the vision of Mary Grey and numerous other Christians and non-Christians who held a vision of the sacredness of the natural world. I begin to long for a vision that would counter the forces of destruction represented in the felling of that silver birch tree and sustain me from being crushed by my growing realization of the grip of corporate greed on our world and its threat to my soul. Mary writes,

> Losing our place in this process has meant loss of our rightful ecstatic capacity, that feeding and being fed by nature's regenerative cycles which gives social living its potential for happiness. This blockage has meant substituting pseudo-gratifications for intimacy, fulfilment of desire and visions of transformation.[1]

The oozing sap from the tree felt like an encounter with the crucified Christ whom we are told bled both blood and water. I thought of the words of Matthew 25 where Jesus tells a parable of the Last Judgement, and speaks of how we either ignore or respond to the hungry, the homeless and the alienated. He says, 'just as you did not do it to one of the least of these, you did not do it to me' (Matt. 25.45). I began to realize that my vision had to expand to more than human life, I had to move from a limited anthropocentric vision of the world to a bigger more inclusive vision. To begin to see myself as just part of one species in a world inhabited by millions of other species. As Anne Primavesi writes,

> We need to make a conscious transition from such perceptions of myself to a perception of my being an earth-centred human, I need to relate to earth *as if* my whole existence depends on that relationship. I need to relate to my fellow human beings *as if* our earth lineage were as central to our being alive as are our human genealogies.[2]

As I began to think, read more and be inspired by others in this new vision I began to feel a powerful motivation from within to do more to protect and nurture the natural world that people like Rupert were teaching me to love.

Visions motivate us

Visions can inspire us to take action, and over the years I have been inspired by the vision of people in movements to bring about social change, such as the Civil Rights Movement, the Suffragettes and more latterly Extinction Rebellion. But complementing this further is my Christian vision that holds that a renewed earth is possible. It has become obvious to me that the predominant and shallow vision held by those in political and economic power – that we will achieve progress by putting our trust in the market and promoting economic growth to the detriment of all else – is leading us towards what many are now calling the sixth mass extinction. Frighteningly, we don't heed the science and we continue with 'business as usual'. Many younger people are in despair because they see no future in a much hotter dystopian world. Younger friends are choosing not to have children as they fear for their future. I want to argue against such fatalism and suggest they are right to feel despondent if they continue to be held by the power of the present individualistic and competitive narrative. For what is leading to despair is a lack of vision.

I'm not sure that we need to discover a new vision, but rather believe we need to recover older narratives that are community based, inclusive and sustainable. For communities to be built, to thrive and be sustainable, a compelling vision and shared narrative must be bought into.

In April 2019, like some medieval army, Extinction Rebellion raised its multicoloured flags in Oxford Street, central London. But this was an army with no weapons, firmly committed to non-violence, peaceful transformation and with a vision of an earth transformed. The vision was spurred on by three clear demands:

1 The Government tell the truth about the existential threat caused by climate breakdown.
2 The Government declare a climate emergency and commit to net zero greenhouse gas emissions by 2030.
3 Citizens' Assemblies be established and be the guiding force for all government decision-making.

Throughout the heady year of 2019, Extinction Rebellion grew in strength, thousands took to the streets, and I was one of hundreds inspired to be arrested. In November 2019, Theresa May's government even declared a Climate Emergency. The year 2020 and the coming of Covid-19 saw a stagnation in Extinction Rebellion's progress, and it has failed to become the mass movement so needed to protect our fragile earth. History will judge whether this was because of a lack of broad-based appeal, an antagonistic media often owned by climate-change deniers, poor strategy or a lack of a compelling vision.

Though it hasn't become the mass movement it hoped to be, the vision of Extinction Rebellion continues to inspire. Joanna Macy, peace activist and deep ecologist, writes, 'When we see with new eyes, we recognize how every action has significance, how the bigger story of the Great Turning is made up of countless smaller stories of communities, campaigns, and personal actions.'[3] The most committed and resilient activists and rebels I've had the pleasure to be alongside all have a long view of history and see themselves in a long line inspired by other activists. The 'Freedom Riders' breaking down segregated buses as part of the US Civil Rights Movement, anti-apartheid demonstrators, and in my own land the Tolpuddle Martyrs and the Suffragettes are often looked to for inspiration. The people who seem to endure longest in the struggle for justice are those with strong spiritual convictions and a long-term vision of a world restored by peace and justice. Martin Luther King's vision and his steadfastness were grounded in his Christian faith:

> The greatest of all virtues is love. Here we find the true meaning of the Christian faith and of the cross. Calvary is the telescope through which we look into the long vista of eternity and see the love of God breaking into time.[4]

Expanding vision

Thirteen years living in the Pilsdon Community and 16 years living at Hilfield Franciscan Community, both in rural Dorset, nurtured in me a new vision that was more communal, regenerative and joyful.

At Pilsdon, I slowly began to feel one with the fields, trees and hills that surrounded the place, and the new experience of hand-milking cows, mucking out pigs, collecting still-warm eggs from the chicken house and days spent digging, weeding and planting in the garden filled me with a huge sense of enchantment and well-being. I found that being in close contact with the natural world seemed also to deepen and improve my relationships with the people I lived with. As Shakespeare said, 'One touch of nature makes the whole world kin.'[5] Out of this intense and growing love for creation I began to more deeply reflect on what a vision of the earth restored might look like.

The longer I lived with the land, the more I began to intuit this and began to see myself not just as part of humanity but belonging to a much bigger, more complex and beautiful system of life.

I also began to be a lot more discerning about what I used my chainsaw for. When I first passed my test, I just wanted to fell trees and accumulate firewood for the community; now I thought a lot more about whether the tree really needed felling, what damage its felling might do to other trees and if taking it out might benefit others around it. Somebody also told me that before felling a tree, Native Americans would thank the tree for all the life it had supported. A new reverence was slowly taking hold of me, learning to resist the comparatively recent post-Enlightenment thinking that nature was there to be exploited by humans and fuel economic growth, and returning me to an earlier and humbler vision of people seeing themselves as just one part in the great web of life. On my nightly walk home from the community across the field, I passed a number of mature oak trees and slowly they became my companions. I'd notice the new bud growth in winter, the green leaf of late spring and dead limbs too. Part of me wanted to get my chainsaw out and tidy the tree up and harvest the timber, but I was learning that dead wood supported more life than the living wood. The old foresters' proverb goes: 'Great oaks take 300 years to grow, 300 years to live and 300 years to die.' I also learnt that a mature oak supports over 2,300 species. I was slowly learning to have a more expansive vision of my part in the world and no longer seeing myself right at the centre of it.

The kinship I discovered at Pilsdon has been further deepened into a vision that sees myself as part of God's vibrant and living creation and demands that I be part of Christ's work of reconciling the whole of humanity and all of creation. It's a big vision inspiring me, towering over and sheltering me just like a mighty oak. If someone asks me to join a well-thought-out non-violent protest seeking to protect the earth and I have the time and capacity, I feel I have little choice but to say yes. Groups like Christian Climate Action (CCA) exist and continue to be sustained not just by the call to protest and act prophetically but the underlying vision of the Peaceable Kingdom envisioned by the prophet Isaiah: 'They will not hurt or destroy on all my holy mountain; for the earth will be full of the knowledge of the LORD as the waters cover the sea (Isa. 11.9).

CCA aligns itself with social justice movements of the past to take part in acts of public witness, non-violent protest and civil disobedience, but its roots lie in the radical witness of Jesus, biblical inspiration and the many strands of the Christian tradition that call for peace, justice and the integrity of God's creation.

A Franciscan vision

Living in the Franciscan community at Hilfield Friary has further stirred up and grounded such a vision for me and the thousands of people who pass through our doors, pray in our chapel, walk in our fields. Many of our visitors comment on both the peaceful and the vital atmosphere of the place. At the root of this is our desire to live out a way of life inspired by Francis of Assisi (1180–1226). Francis was the son of a wealthy cloth merchant. Following a year-long imprisonment after fighting in the battle of Collestrada, an encounter with a leper, and hearing the voice of Christ in the church of St Damiano he chose a life of renunciation and total simplicity. Francis rejected a life of wealth and privilege and chose the life of an itinerant preacher, depending on simple manual labour or begging to provide for his needs. Dramatically, his father called him before the Bishop of Assisi to try to talk some sense into his son, but Francis' response was to strip naked in front of his father and hand back his clothes to him saying, 'I have but one father and that is my Father in heaven.' At the heart of Francis' vision was a desire to follow Christ by living a life so simple that it would lead him to live from a place of gratitude and total dependence on God. He was against the order possessing property as he argued that if the Brothers had property, they'd take up arms to defend it. Rather, the Brothers, through their poverty and associated humility, would be in a better position to be peacemakers.

Despite the precarious nature of the life of a mendicant friar, the Franciscan order inspired people to become friars in great numbers. From its founding in 1210 with 12 members, by 1220 there were 5,000 friars in southern Europe and beyond. The vision of Francis still captures the imaginations of many today and his condemnation of wealth, his solidarity with the marginalized, his peacemaking, his sense of kinship with creation are all desperately needed in our fractured, individualistic and consumerist world. It's no surprise that Francis is often referred to as 'the patron saint of ecology'.

Keeping the vision alive

What continues to inspire people to join Hilfield Community as friars or lay members is an 800-year-old vision of a man who wanted to live more like Jesus. Hilfield Friary was founded in 1921 by Brother Giles, an Anglican Franciscan who was working with the homeless in Oxford. He had a dream of providing a safe place in the countryside where homeless men could come and stay for a few weeks or months to have a chance of rebuilding their lives. In 1921 there were over 70,000 tramping the roads of Britain, many of them discharged from the army, and a large number of whom would have been suffering from what was then called 'shellshock', which we would now refer to as post-traumatic stress disorder. A year after founding the community, Giles left in disgrace and public humiliation after he'd been seen kissing another man. The work could have ended there, but Brother Douglas, who shared Giles' vision, arrived to bring vigour and great compassion to the new friary, providing respite for what he described as wayfarers and a chance for people to rebuild their lives in a safe and well-ordered community.

For 85 years, Hilfield provided shelter and a place at our common table for wayfarers and people in recovery from addiction and poor mental health, but by 2005 a lack of Brothers meant the friary would either have to close or be reimagined. Fortunately, Brother Sam had a vision of the friary becoming a mixed community of friars and lay people, with a particular emphasis on conservation and eco-spirituality. He envisaged a community that would seek to live simply and sustainably with a sense of reverence for God's creation, and that would rediscover Francis of Assisi's commitment to all the creatures of the earth. The new community would seek to highlight the climate emergency caused by the continued burning of fossil fuels and the loss of biodiversity caused by our lack of care for our common home. Fortunately, others captured Sam's vision, and the friary was able to reinvent itself and attract new people to join.

I'm pleased to say that the friary now warmly welcomes a rich diversity of people. We have community members from Ghana, Korea, Botswana, the Solomon Islands, most parts of Europe and North America. We share a common commitment to a life of prayer, a simple sustainable life, the welcome of visitors, and the care of our 45 acres of land. The work with the marginalized continues with community members going out to work with Gypsies and Travellers, prisoners and asylum seekers.

Inspired by the vision of St Francis and those who followed in the tradition, we continue to work the land, welcome a wide variety of visitors and maintain the practice of fourfold daily prayers. People keep returning to the friary, because it is a physically beautiful and peaceful location – the only noise pollution you might hear is the chug of the occasional tractor – but more so because of the sense of belonging they don't find anywhere else. It's a belonging to the landscape, trees and creatures that surround us but also a sense of belonging to God and each other. A year before his death, Francis wrote his 'Canticle of the Creatures', probably the first poem to be written in Italian vernacular in his local Umbrian dialect. The Canticle sings of a vision of fraternity and sorority, speaking of Brother Sun, Sister Moon, Brother Fire, Sister Water, Mother Earth. It speaks too of Francis' longing for reconciliation between people and befriending of Sister Death. The poem above all speaks of a vision of belonging to this earth of which we are a part and our interdependence on our fellow creatures and our need for reconciliation with the earth, each other and our creator. Simon Cocksedge writes,

> Francis' example points us towards constantly choosing non-possessive peaceful relationship and reconciliation between humanity, creation and God in everything we do. Additionally, it encourages us routinely to see God and God's loving gifts throughout creation, and so to live in joy, praise and thankfulness. These are key Franciscan themes.[6]

Rather magically, Chantal Muller, a long-term member of the community, has created a sensory Canticle Garden through which you are encouraged to take off your shoes and meditatively walk. The light of Brother Sun shines through a rounded hole in a slab of Portland stone, a crescent Sister Moon gleams out from a mirror mosaic on the ground. You can walk through a Sister Water feature and smell and touch Mother Earth as you crush thymes and chamomile plants on your journey round the garden and listen to Sister Air as a wind chime sculpture gently clangs in the wind.

Having less brings us more

Francis' life was full of symbolic actions that expressed his vision of a more just and joyful world. He lived at a time of great conflict between the old feudal nobility and the new merchant classes and constant battles between newly formed city states. The church of his day also tended to side with the ruling classes and had grown wealthy and complacent. Francis' life of radical poverty, as symbolized by his Brothers wearing the simple rough tunic of a labourer, which later became the habit, was a direct challenge to church leaders' love of power, wealth and status. If you visit the Basilica in Assisi you can see displayed in a case his woollen habit, which is a coat of multiple patches suggesting many repairs. Repair was at the heart of Francis' call, having heard the voice of Jesus speaking to him from the cross in the tumbledown chapel of St Damiano saying, 'Repair my Church'. Francis took the voice literally and began to buy stone to restore church buildings but gradually came to understand that it was about the repair of relationships, in society and between people and God. He would often give his cloak away if he found a poor man without one, saying that the cloak had only been given to him on loan until he found someone in greater need.

Relinquishment was at the heart of Francis' vision. Like those in the Deep Adaptation Movement, Francis knew that the unrestrained pursuit of wealth led to violence, fear and the diminishment of human life. He knew that the amassing of needless wealth tended to separate people from each other and God and that true security was to be found in the quality of our relationships with each other and the living world. His Brothers were forbidden to travel by horse, always having to walk – as he knew from his days as a soldier that riding a horse gave you a sense of power and separated you from those below you. Speed, efficiency, autonomy and control were let go of and replaced by fraternity, solidarity and mutual support. Today at Hilfield we seek to walk to the bus stop which links with our train station, and consciously limit and share any car journeys we need to make. Walking to a place, while always the slowest option, is also the most joyful and the way you're most likely to meet others. Several times when we've been cut off by snow, I've accompanied people on the three-mile walk to our nearest station, always taking a couple of stout sticks to keep us upright. They've always been joyous journeys through the whitened and muffled landscape, and friendship tested by the challenging environment has been deepened. Yes, a vision of less when lived out practically so often brings us more and certainly builds up our common life in contrast to the prevailing culture of accumulation that makes us fearful of others who might take what we've got; or if we don't have what others have, it can lead to a sense of lack and lead to anxiety and poor self-esteem. Having less can encourage us to ask for help and encourages the sharing of resources. At the heart of the climate and biodiversity crisis is a philosophy that promotes consumption and the creation of excess with little regard for our common home.

What an ecological or Franciscan vision offers is a sustainable economic model based on having less material goods, more public sharing and the strengthening of mutual bonds with interdependence replacing independence, reverence for the earth replacing narcissism and gratitude replacing self-sufficiency.

Vision binds us together

Vision is something that can shape and hold a community and bind people together in hard times. Religious belief at its best can be something to galvanize people in a sense of community. The Latin root *religo* means to bind people, and though at times ossified, sectarian and too often siding with the rich and powerful, religious groups definitely endure, and much of this is due to their founding inspiration. The words of the Buddha, the teachings of Christ, the wisdom of the Hebrew prophets, sutras of the

Holy Koran, the poetry of the Upanishads all continue to provide the reader and devotee with resources to grapple with the question, 'How should we live now?' Religious belief is above all rooted in the communal, the 'ummah', the 'body of Christ', the Dharma, the people of the Covenant. Religious rituals, communal prayer, times of pilgrimage are all part of holding people together in a sense of common purpose.

There is a constant temptation in Christianity to dilute the challenging and inclusive vision of the kingdom of God proclaimed by Jesus with its radical equality, inclusion and voluntary poverty. Too often the voice of pragmatism has won out over that of vision, and Christianity has chosen to be a part of Empire and colonizing top-down narratives. Archbishop Desmond Tutu, with a twinkle in his eye, would say to Western Christians, 'When your missionaries first came, they had the Bible and we had the land; we closed our eyes to pray and when we opened them we had the Bible and you had the land!' I sometimes despair about how my own church loves to side with the rich and powerful. But if I look at the history of Christianity it is full of movements that seek to recover its radical traditions, particularly those who chose to live in community.

At the end of the third century when the Emperor Constantine had converted to Christianity, it became the state religion and went from a persecuted minority to a ruling majority. In response to this, certain men and women retreated to the Egyptian and Palestinian deserts seeking to challenge Christianity's adoption by the state. They were known as the Desert Mothers and Fathers and led lives of relinquishment, seeking to return to a simpler and more authentic life, seeking to recapture the vision of the Early Church.

Over the years they began to live communally in monasteries, which were a communal challenge to a world dominated by empires and princely kingdoms based on military power and the politics of divide and rule. Monastic life was systematized under the Rule of Benedict in the sixth century and for centuries their communal life was an alternative non-violent vision and way of life in contrast to the rule by force of the European powers around them. Benedictine monks following the Rule would live a carefully balanced life with regular communal prayer, study and simple manual work, all practised within the enclosure of the monastery. Other orders began to form who felt the Benedictine life was becoming too comfortable, such as the Carthusians, the Cistercians and the Carmelites. The Franciscan and the Dominican orders grew up as orders of preachers who moved from place to place rather than living in the enclosure of a monastery. The Reformation brought an end to this communal life in Britain; 15,000 monks were pensioned off and community lands were appropriated by the state. This way of life was thus lost until its revival in the mid nineteenth century.

Little Gidding and inspiration

Before that, there was an attempt to revive a particular kind of English religious life. In 1625 Nicholas Ferrar MP, a member of the Virginia Company that was establishing colonies in America, who was tipped to be the next Chancellor of the Exchequer, renounced public life, choosing instead to buy a manor house and ten acres of adjoining land at Little Gidding in Huntingdonshire. He had grown tired of the corruption of Parliament and the dominant political, social and cultural values of his day and felt drawn to a vision of something much simpler and God-centred. The community, like the former monasteries, was organized around times of corporate daily prayer, simple manual work and the welcome of visitors. King Charles I visited in all his pomp and then did so again later when on the run, according to T. S. Eliot: 'If you were to come at night like a broken King'.[7] The community lasted until 1652 when it was closed down during the Commonwealth, accused of being an 'Armenian Nunnery'. Today it's best known for its T. S. Eliot connections and as a place 'to kneel where prayer has been made valid'.[8]

On 4 December 2024, I visited for the annual commemoration of Nicholas Ferrar and entered the same church his community would have prayed in. It had changed little since his day, oak-panelled walls, lit by candles and bone-chillingly cold. In a window I read one of Nicholas' favourite sayings, 'It is a good old way keep on it.' I felt myself transported back in time, a feeling so similar to the time I'd picked up Pilsdon Community's only 'relic', a Book of Common Prayer, hand-bound and stitched, with a cover embroidered at Little Gidding, which sits in the oak-panelled Pilsdon house chapel. As the service ended, we moved outside and I laid a wreath on the tomb of Nicholas Ferrar and again was transported back in time, this time recalling Percy Smith, the founder of Pilsdon Community, speaking to camera: 'I stood at the tomb of Nicholas Ferrar and became convinced of the utter sanity of that way of life.' It was at that point Percy had fully captured the vision of Little Gidding, which led to the establishment of Pilsdon. And here was I standing in that tradition.

I think a vision and its variations can be compounded for good. Each year I become more aware of the layers of inspiration that continue to inspire the community at Hilfield. If you looked at it in cross section it might look like different strata of rock, the weight of glory pressing down and producing something beautiful, strong and enduring like a diamond. And yet it's a living thing, fed by various historical, poetic, literary and artistic stimuli. For me, it would be the stories from the New Testament that so inspired Francis. Stories and artistic representation of his life, then those of his followers, including characters like Clare of Assisi.

Visiting the Francis of Assisi Exhibition in the National Gallery (February–June 2023) after an emotionally bruising few days slow marching with Just Stop Oil, being pilloried and jostled and nearly run over by an irate motorist, was both comfort and inspiration. I gazed at Costa's magnificent golden portrait of St Francis standing on a hill outside Assisi, with arms raised ecstatically welcoming the rising sun; it was a reminder of the beauty of the earth we'd been seeking to defend. Black and white footage from Pasorelli's *The Hawks and the Sparrows* film with a dishevelled band of Brothers slowly walking through the rain exactly mirrored the slow march a group of us had made the day before. The picture that moved me most was called *Sacco* and was an abstract made up of layers of hessian punctured by a couple of round red wounds. It was created by Alberto Burri, a former Italian army medic and prisoner of war, and brings the stigmata of St Francis into the suffering of war casualties. It was a further experience of feeling strongly part of the thread of St Francis' vision seeking to inspire compassion linked to the suffering of Christ. Just what I needed to see in my shaky and exhausted state. I left the gallery feeling energized and ready for the next call to civil disobedience.

Just outside the National Gallery is the church of St Martin-in-the-Fields, which was where Brother Douglas used to sleep in the crypt alongside London's homeless when he was up in London in the 1930s, lobbying Parliament for the repeal of the Vagrancy Act. Like Burri, Douglas had been a medic in World War One and, after the war, had come to Hilfield to provide a safe place for those recovering from the trauma of war. In my slightly wounded state I felt lucky to be returning to a Franciscan house still living under the inspiration of characters such as Brother Douglas, Pope Francis and Brother Sam, all living out and building and expanding a Franciscan vision that inspires my daily life.

Drawing strength from a tradition

I've learnt that layered or laminated wood is incredibly strong, so drawing from a tradition can really strengthen and sustain a community. Martin Luther King knew this too and the durability of the Civil Rights Movement in the United States came from deep biblical roots, the inspiration of black spirituality and a focus on non-violence taught by Gandhi. For a community to have a long-term sustainability, the vision has to run deep. Writing about King's vision of the beloved community, Marsh says,

> the contemporary retrievals of the spiritual movements towards 'redemption, reconciliation and the creation of the beloved community' demonstrate the vital role of spiritual nourishment in the work of mercy and justice, not as a substitute for material sustenance but as a condition of justice.[9]

Not all visions that bind people together will lead to justice and peace. At their worst they can bring about wholesale destruction, violence and even genocide. Nazism was rooted in a powerful vision of a Germany transformed, Aryan supremacy, drawing deeply on the German folk movement and the vision of a new kingdom, the Third Reich. It used powerful symbolism to bind people together and mass rallies engendered feelings of solidarity and belonging. The desire for a strong leader seems to be returning with a vengeance, with the growth in populism and leaders with clear simpler answers usually scapegoating vulnerable minorities.

Neo-liberalism, too, which is the predominant vision behind the main economic mantra of 'continuous growth' to deliver the promised land of jobs, freedom, choice and individual wealth we all need, embraced by every Western government, is a vision people keep voting for. Both philosophies are mightily destructive of community, the first in its tendency to polarize, promote blame and build military and internal security services to silence dissent, the second in its destruction of the planet we share as a common home with myriad other species.

Visions that build sustainable ways of life or what King would describe as the 'Beloved Community', are always built on the principles of non-violence. He writes, 'Hatred and bitterness can never cure the disease of fear, only love can do that. Hatred paralyses; love releases it. Hatred confuses life; love harmonises it. Hatred darkens life; love illumines it.'[10] It might be helpful here to think of the contrast between ego- and eco-driven motivations, to help differentiate between constructive and destructive visions. The ego-driven system is all about protecting the individual, driven by the need to accumulate wealth and protect the little that we have and by the fear of the 'other'. Contrastingly, an ecological model is based around understandings of interdependence, reliance on each other – what Archbishop Desmond Tutu described as 'ubuntu' and the sharing of abundant resources.

Contemplative vision

The building and maintenance of such vision needs time and attention; learning to see differently and more expansively is aided by taking time out and embracing a contemplative disposition. Some of Martin Luther King's most inspiring writing came from prison where enforced solitude gave him time for reflection. St Francis only began the Franciscan movement after some years of solitude. In my first year at Hilfield I remember questioning why the Franciscan house in Worcestershire was called Glasshampton Monastery. 'Shouldn't it be a friary; aren't friars supposed to be outwardly looking?' Someone gently explained to me that there was a strong contemplative side to St Francis who often spent weeks in solitude and even had his own 'Rules for Hermits'. Since then, I've discovered the more contemplative dimension to Franciscan spirituality. It's perhaps best summed up in the life of Clare of Assisi, one of Francis' first followers and a continual inspiration to him. In her second letter to Agnes of Prague she succinctly sums up the contemplative life: 'Gaze, consider, contemplate, imitate.'[11]

Since that conversation, I've helped build a prayer hut and hermitage on wheels as an expression of Hilfield's commitment to a more reflective life.

Franciscan Richard Rohr speaks of the need to recover this contemplative vision by promoting what he calls *Visio Divina*. Many are familiar with *Lectio Divina*, a way of reading Scripture contemplatively, but Rohr suggests we also need to recover a practice of reading nature slowly and contemplatively to learn to look and look again. This in turn will nurture a wider vision.

To develop and renew vision we need to take time out. Waiting for it means it's more likely to come from a sense of the common good rather than being driven by ego. As Simone Weil regularly stressed, 'The most precious gifts don't come to us by going in search of them but by waiting for them.'[12]

Regular time out each day, and establishing a quieter more reflective day each month, can be a way of nurturing vision. How we protect it and seek to live it out by providing structures to contain it is what we shall turn to next.

Questions

1. What parts of the New Testament are particularly visionary?
2. What do you find attractive about the Franciscan vision?
3. Who has inspired you by their vision, and which visions capture your imagination?
4. What might be your vision of a renewed new earth?
5. How do you make sure a church or organization sticks to its vision?

Practical suggestions

1. Learn more about St Francis.
2. Look at some of the writing of contemporary Franciscan Friar Richard Rohr on the Centre for Action and Contemplation website: www.cac.org.
3. Write down your vision for a better world.
4. Think about joining or supporting an organization that corresponds to your vision.
5. Consider risking doing something that feels difficult but is in line with your vision and principles.
6. Refuse to give in to narratives of despair; like Wendell Berry, ‘practise resurrection’.
7. Practise *Visio Divina*, looking and looking again at something and embedding gratitude into your life.

Notes

1 Mary Grey, 2004, *Sacred Longings*, London: SCM Press, p. 20.

2 Anne Primavesi, 2003, *Gaia's Gift: Earth, Ourselves and God after Copernicus*, Abingdon: Routledge, p. 82.

3 Joanna Macy and Chris Johnstone, 2012, *Active Hope*, Novato, CA: New World Library, p. 198.

4 Martin Luther King, 1974, *Strength to Love*, London: Hodder and Stoughton, p. 146.

5 William Shakespeare, *Troilus and Cressida*, Act 3, Scene 3.

6 Simon Cocksedge, Samuel Double, Nicholas Alan Worssam, 2021, *Seeing Differently*, London: Canterbury Press, p. 67.

7 T. S. Eliot, 1952, *Four Quartets*, London: Faber and Faber, p. 36.

8 Eliot, *Four Quartets*, p. 36.

9 Charles Marsh, 2006, *The Beloved Community*, New York: Basic Books, 2006, p. 65.

10 Martin Luther King, 1974, *Strength to Love*, London: Hodder and Stoughton, p. 122.

11 Clare of Assisi, 1993, 'Second Letter to Agnes of Prague' in Regis J. Armstrong, ed., *Clare of Assisi: Early Documents*, New York: Franciscan Institute Publications, p. 42.

12 Simone Weil, 2009, *Waiting on God*, Abingdon: Routledge, p. 35.

3

Boundaries

The alarm wakes me; it's still dark in the cottage and pulling on my milking clothes helps me move from sleep into the beginnings of a new day. Slipping into my wellies, I gently close the door on my sleeping household, walk down the lane to the little footbridge and cross the stream that borders the community land. I click open the wooden gate and head eastwards across the field looking up towards the hill, known as Pilsdon Pen, and seeing the first hint of light forming out of the darkness.

As I reach the next gate leading into the vegetable garden, I pause and listen to the silence, then I'm on through the vegetable garden rustling along in my Gore-Tex trousers. I collect buckets and some hot water from the dairy and nod a greeting to Henry, who is already scooping nuts from the feed bin and pouring them into the stone troughs at each end of the little milking parlour. I go out and rattle the back gate, calling the cows as I do so: 'Hayoo!, Hayoo!' and out of the darkness I see their lumbering shapes and hear them slosh through the muddy path towards the field's edge.

I open the gate and they're quickly into the parlour. We chain their necks as their heads dive down into the nuts. Then it's a quick wash of Dahlia's udders with warm towels, a dip of the fingers in the greasy udder salve, a tuck of the milking stool down under their flanks, a first squeeze of each teat onto the floor to check for mastitis, then the rhythmic compression and tugging of the teats as milk jets into the bucket. I huddle into the cow, feeling its warmth, and my hands are soon warmed by the flow of the milk through the teats. There's a low rumbling in my ear. The cow's rumen is busy digesting last night's grass. I can hear Henry's low singing to Angelica on the other side of the parlour. We're soon finished, release the cows back into the field and, as Henry brushes the parlour, I carry down two buckets of steaming creamy milk to the dairy. Already someone is there, and I can hear the pasteurizer warming up. I see the glow of a cigarette outside the back of the house and sit down next to Trevor, he with his first fag of the day, me with my first tea. For a few minutes we sit in companionable silence watching the light get stronger over Pilsdon Pen.

I hear the church bell and move towards the church for Morning Prayer. I pause in the porch and undertake the ritual of taking off my hat and wellies, recognizing I'm entering a sacred space. I sit on one of the straw bales that line the walls of the small medieval church and wait as several others assemble. We slowly work through a simple liturgy of prayers, and a singing bowl is sounded to help contain a few minutes of silence, sounding again to mark its ending. Then the kitchen bell rings to call the community to breakfast. I collect my fried egg and beans and sit down and eat. Then it's time for the morning meeting, where the framework of the day is planned and much information exchanged. Today in the garden we're weeding and preparing beds for planting cabbages and other brassicas. At 11am, a bell rings to announce the mid-morning break where people gather for coffee and biscuits, then back to the garden. At 12.40pm the church bell rings for midday prayers, then the lunch bell brings people quickly into the large dining room for grace and the sound of chairs being pulled out as people sit and eat. I move to the library for a short look at the papers and a doze, then it's an afternoon of splitting and stacking logs. We take tea and toast in the common room, lit by a blazing fire with logs taken from the previous year's stack. I'm back under Dahlia again when someone looks over the wall and warns, 'A pair of wayfarers have turned up; I think you need to go and see them.'

The rhythm of my lovely peaceful day has been interrupted; I sense trouble ahead. I quickly finish milking, leaving Henry to finish up, and walk into the common room. To my surprise I see two women, who look to be in their 40s. Out of the hundreds of wayfarers who come on foot to Pilsdon it's rare to see women unless they're referred to us from an agency in advance. My intuition is telling me to be careful and, unusually, I introduce myself formally as Jonathan, the community leader. I ask them their names and when one of them introduces herself as Jesus, my intuition shouts, 'Watch out.' I turn to the other who I'm sure is going to be called Peter, but she is calling herself Joy. Jesus explains with bright eyes that they're on a mission to save the people of the world and God has told them to come to Pilsdon.

I ask, 'Where's home?'

When they reply, 'Wherever people welcome us', an inner voice starts screaming at me, 'Get rid of them!'

That week had been a tough week with one of our long-term guests having to be sectioned in the local psychiatric hospital, and the arrival of two other very vulnerable people. I firmly explain to Jesus and Joy that we don't have any accommodation for women who are wayfarers, which is true, although we can always find a bed – even if it's a mattress on a floor – if people are in real need.

I suggest they go to Bristol where there is much more emergency accommodation at places like the Salvation Army, and let them know that if we go now, I can get them on a train. I quickly persuade them into a car and have a long 20 minutes of a very disgruntled Jesus telling me that the website says nothing about wayfarers needing to be men, and we're a very poor example of a Christian community, and at the end of the world and at the final judgement we will be condemned unless we change our ways. I buy tickets for Bristol and am relieved to leave them behind.

But driving back I'm haunted by the thought, 'You turned Jesus away.'

Pulling into the yard I hear the bell going for evening prayer and welcome some time to sit quietly in the church. After supper, I go and do a bit of admin in the office, and then the final bell rings for night prayer in the tiny house chapel and I begin to let go of the day, as we repeat the phrase, 'Into your hands, O Lord, I commend my spirit.'

That day contains so many different boundaries that give our common life at Pilsdon a sense of shape. The crossing from sleep to wakefulness, the fences around the community land, the daily rhythms of milking, bells ringing for church, the singing bowl to contain corporate silence, the fixed points of meal times, work time, leisure time. Then, more dramatically, the need I feel to enforce the boundary of exclusion, in order to protect the community.

At Pilsdon, as in a traditional monastery, life happens between the bells, which give an order to the place, mark time and summon people to gather for prayer and food. For many of our guests, their former lives had been chaotic with little formal structure. Drinking, drug use, mental illness and homelessness had reduced many to living in a state of constant disruption. Sleep was more likely to happen in the day than in the night, particularly if you'd been sleeping rough in a town where it was much safer to sleep in a warm library or a sunny park than risk being attacked in a doorway in the dark. For those living with depression, getting out of bed or the flat was a big challenge. We insisted at Pilsdon that people come to lunch and the evening meal and if someone was absent, their door would be knocked on and they'd be summoned to the meal if well enough. Not everyone found it easy sitting down to eat at a table after sometimes years of solitary eating; for others it was a huge comfort to be surrounded by a large extended family. Great care was taken over the preparation of food and meals as we saw eating together as a core expression of our community life, and if someone was missing, we would be incomplete as a community. Though there was rigidity around attendance, there was always elasticity when it came to inviting unexpected visitors to eat with us. There always had to be enough for second helpings and a newly arrived guest.

So many people now eat on their own or in front of a television or other device, choosing what they watch, what they eat and when they eat it, but I always enjoy entering the refectory at the friary often not knowing what the meal will be, but aware that I'll have company and an interesting conversation with a new guest or longstanding community member. The discipline of the common table allows us to meet and engage with new people and deepen friendship with those we've known for years. A number of our guests at Hilfield live alone and the opportunity to share food with others and share in the drying up afterwards is profoundly restorative for many. Each meal is begun with a short prayer of thanksgiving and the evening meal is ended with a short reading and prayers for all who have lived at Hilfield, specifically naming a few who have lived here in the recent past and prayers for those who are away from us. Over my years at Hilfield I've been away in some fairly risky situations and knowing the community is praying for me gives a great sense of reassurance and belonging. Though away from the community I still feel held by it.

Like Pilsdon, life at Hilfield is ordered by bells, but even more so. We have a huge two-tonne bell at the entrance, which sounds a ten-minute warning before prayer times and can be heard from a mile away. There's an Angelus bell rung just before the service begins and a bell rung to summon people to mealtimes.

Keith, a neurologically diverse man who lived 67 years at Hilfield, was responsible for ringing the mealtime bells, which suited his very ordered view of how life should be, and the regular discipline of the friary allowed him to feel safe and contained. 'I keep law and order round here,' he used to joke, but there was a truth about it, as he was always on time and kept the whole community on track with his faithful bell-ringing. He welcomed every new visitor to the friary with a childlike simplicity, and always with the same questions: 'What is your name?' and then, 'Where are you from?' And he remembered who you were and where you were from if you visited again. As well as ringing the bell, he'd put out the rubbish, collect the recycling bins, put jugs of water on the table for every meal. He was happy and content in his routine but if it was disrupted, if we changed the time of a meal, for example, or dinner was late or the bin men failed to turn up, he could be quickly enraged. It was as if the security of his world was threatened. To an extent, I think we're all a bit like Keith. We all need the security of routines to help us feel safe and give a sense of pattern and order in an increasingly disrupted world. The genius of Benedictine life is to recognize this.

Benedictine spirituality

The Latin word for rule is 'trellis', which in gardening is a structure that supports a plant and allows it to grow and find its own way while benefitting from something to hang on to. Written in the sixth century when the Roman Empire was facing collapse, the Rule of Benedict is credited by some historians with holding the fabric of Western civilization together and has much to continue to teach us today.

In the prologue to his rule, Benedict writes, 'We wish not to impose anything too harsh or burdensome.'[1] The rule is about maintaining a well-balanced life, full of moderation, that leads to a deeper sense of joy. In a world that was in danger of falling apart, Benedict had a vision of a well-ordered community life that was an antidote to an uncertain future. Today we don't so much need a new St Benedict to come and inspire us but rather a recovery of his simple well-boundaried way based on love and placing our spiritual life at the centre. So strong are the forces of consumerism, militarism and hyper-individualism that are destroying societies across the world, that only well-disciplined, resilient communities with strong guiding principles can stand up to them. As Michael Northcott writes,

> Every action, every community, every household that turns away from heedless consumption towards mindful care and compassionate use of earth and space and to just reward for labour and craft of other persons, contributes to the necessary recovery of this vision.[2]

In his rule, Benedict is clear that strong boundaries are there for the good of all, however harsh they may sometimes seem: 'The good of all concerned, however, may prompt us to a little strictness in order to amend faults and safeguard love.'[3]

Globally, since the almost unquestioning adoption of neo-liberal economics in the early 1980s, there has been a great emphasis on deregulation of economies and blind trust in the free market. There has been a trust that the market will sort things out and state intervention is something to be avoided as it will hamper and slow economic growth.

Groups such as trade unions and environmental regulators were portrayed as the enemies of prosperity and wealth creation. The boundaries of red tape needed cutting and financial controls on currency and trading were seen as limiting economic growth. State assets were privatized in the belief that private companies would run water, electricity and transport more efficiently. In 2008, the lack of regulation and control of risk on the USA sub-prime mortgage market led to a major financial crisis which was only mitigated by strong state intervention. In the UK, this meant the effective nationalization of two major banks. The heavily polluted state of UK rivers and coastal water with the regular discharge of sewage is a powerful metaphor of where deregulation can leave us. The lack of investment in vital sewage infrastructure at the expense of paying dividends to shareholders has led to many UK rivers and beaches now being polluted by human waste.

> When you create something that is a naturalised geographical monopoly you need really careful and effective regulation, because by definition the companies are set up to take advantage. Instead, you've got 30 years of political indifference and regulatory failure. And guess what? In that vacuum the water companies, financed by venture capital, completely game the system.[4]

Kate Raworth, in her book *Doughnut Economics*, offers an alternative way of doing economics that restores the idea of setting limits on economic growth. The image of the doughnut sees economics operating in the space between social and environmental boundaries. It is an economics that imposes limits and suggests sustainable post-growth economies.

Following World War Two and the horrors of the Holocaust, the killing of civilians through the Blitz, the carpet bombing of German cities and the nuclear catastrophe that obliterated the Japanese cities of Hiroshima and Nagasaki, the United Nations was established and there was an attempt to limit this kind of indiscriminate killing and violence. The Universal Declaration of Human Rights adopted by the United Nations on 10 December

1948 and the promotion of international law, with such institutions as the International Criminal Court, was an attempt to limit the suffering of innocent civilians. It's impossible to know to what extent these humanitarian institutions have limited the killing of individuals, but it is becoming clear that their influence is being eroded. The Rule of Benedict, with its emphasis on setting limits on our community life, is needed now more than ever.

Setting limits

In all the world's major religions we are taught to recognize unhealthy desires and learn to curb their demands on us. Only in recognizing, naming and facing our addictions will we ever be free of them. At the heart of this is an understanding that only regular and ordered spiritual practices can free us from the wild hunger of self-destructive tendencies. In Buddhism the call to be released from false attachments, and to take refuge in the Buddha, is a powerful renunciation of the narrative that security will come through self-reliance and the accumulation of property. In Judaism, the weekly practice of keeping the Sabbath is a direct contradiction of deregulation. The Sabbath is bounded by the coming of darkness at its beginning and end, and the cessation of work for 24 hours. As such, it reminds us of the need for rest and the fundamental truth that it is God in control of our destiny and not our unlimited appetites in the 'city that never sleeps'.

As Bruggeman stresses,

> Sabbath is the practical ground for breaking the power of acquisitiveness and for creating a public will for an accent on restraint. Sabbath is the cessation of widely shared practices of acquisitiveness. It provides time, space and energy for coming to the ultimate recognition that more commodities do not satisfy. Sabbath is variously restraint, withdrawal or divestment from the concrete practices of society that specialise in anxiety.[5]

In Judaism, Christianity and Islam, the practice of fasting is a direct challenge to consumption without limits. At Hilfield, in the season of Lent, as a community we agree to fast. Every Thursday evening in Lent we fast from any electronic devices – that means no phones, TVs or laptops. Instead, we gather together for an evening of conversation.

Thomas McCarthy, an Irish Traveller and folk singer, told me how somebody proudly presented his grandfather in Ireland with what was then a fairly new invention called a 'wireless'. Neighbours gathered round to listen to the radio, but after an hour or so his grandad abruptly stood up switched off the radio and shouted, 'Get that thing out of here, it's a conversation killer.' He realized, with great prescience, the power of technology to break down community. During Lent at Hilfield, we often change our eating habits. One year we only ate food grown in the UK, and for me this was like going back to my childhood, lots of pies, potatoes and lots of apples. The rest of the year we seek to limit what we eat by only consuming meat we have grown on the farm, or shot locally, and we have a rule that we only eat three meat-based meals a week. This recognizes the enormous cost to the planet of the over-consumption of meat.

I was privileged to be in the West Bank in the Holy Month of Ramadan and impressed by the immense corporate solidarity built by the communal fast. Every Muslim over the age of ten, unless they had special medical needs, abstained from food, water, coffee and cigarettes from sunrise to sunset. It was strange visiting Palestinian friends and not being welcomed with tea, coffee and food, which is so much part of their culture of hospitality, but this was replaced by a deeper sense of kinship in the discipline of the fast. There was also a shared joy in the Iftar, the breaking of the fast at dusk, and the eating together was done in a spirit of gratitude.

The rationing that went on in World War Two, the rationing we voluntarily practise at Hilfield Friary, the communal fasting of Islam – all these offer a source of joy and kinship when shared together. All the great religious traditions insist that the limitation of our appetites and the stripping away of possessions and external securities will lead us to a deeper sense of joy and dependence on the true source of life. In Hinduism there's a tradition of renunciation of material goods called *sannyasa* and it is embodied in the yellow-clad Sannyasis who, in the tradition, once they have seen their sons' sons born, renounce the world and become wandering ascetics. In Buddhism, the Pali word *nekkhamma* suggests a turning from the world of desire and leading a holy life. Jesus teaches his followers not to worry about what they will eat or wear:

> Look at the birds of the air; they neither sow nor reap nor gather into barns, and yet your heavenly Father feeds them ... Consider the lilies of the field, how they grow; they neither toil nor spin, yet I tell you, even Solomon in all his glory was not clothed like one of these. (Matt. 6.26–9)

Less is more.

'Taxation' is a way of reducing the wealth of some for the benefit of others, but has become a dirty word as it limits people's ability to spend their money on what they want to buy and is portrayed as theft from hard-working people. It's tantamount to electoral suicide for a party to promise to raise taxes for the common good. But what's wrong with limiting personal wealth if it leads to the common wealth of the whole community?

Campaigns for divestment from fossil fuel companies are a sign of pushback against a model that puts profit and maximum returns for shareholders as the only way of doing economics. Since 2019, the Church Commissioners, the Church of England Pensions Board and all the dioceses of the Church of England have divested from fossil fuels, as well as no longer investing in similarly death-dealing commodities such as arms manufacturers or tobacco.

No longer investing in highly profitable fossil fuel companies is a sign of setting the limits we need if our world community is to reimagine more sustainable ways of living within our limits. Community life teaches us that there are limits and it's OK to run out, not have things and share our limited resources. At Hilfield there are people who have a great concern that we'll run out of milk, which I think is a real deep-rooted mammalian fear of hunger. We don't rush out to the supermarket but will pick up milk the next time somebody goes into town. We justify this by saying we've guests to look after, so the rule of hospitality trumps the rule of living more simply.

We've taken a corporate decision to source our milk from a local very ethical dairy farm, called Liberty Dairies. While the milk is more expensive, we know exactly where it comes from. Their cows live outdoors on organic grazing and are only milked once a day. This is in huge contrast to a big commercial dairy farm where cows are permanently kept indoors, fed with silage (fermented grass or maize) and milked three times a day. The milk will be collected by tanker, driven many miles to a processing plant, and then distributed in plastic bottles to a supermarket. Pete delivers our milk in stainless steel churns twice a week and we dispense it into sterilized glass bottles for the table.

Hard boundaries and negotiated boundaries

In January 2024 Hilfield planted a new 200-metre hedge in partnership with the St Ethelburga's Centre for Reconciliation and Peace 'Lifelines' project. 'Lifelines' was established in 2022 with the vision to connect farmers and faith groups and to plant hedgerow, particularly on land that has been industrially farmed. One of the main landowners targeted was the Church Commissioners, who manage 100,000 acres of land, much of which is intensively cultivated. Planting new hedgerow is the quickest way of restoring and enhancing biodiversity into the landscape. Hedges provide natural corridors and shelter, food and protection for birds and small mammals. They can also increase crop yields by protecting from wind and soil erosion and are good natural boundaries.

The new hedge we planted has ten different species in it and over a 1,000 little plants snake for 200 metres up the road. It's mulched with woodchip for the first half, and then on the second half the mulch at the base of the plants, used for supressing weeds and keeping the moisture in, is wool from our sheep and one of our neighbour's flock. Appropriately, the field it bounds is often full of sheep in their thick winter coats.

Hedge planting really took off following the enclosure of the commons and they were used to delineate the new landowners' rights, which let the commoners know they no longer had any rights to grazing or for the collection of timber for firewood. The enclosures are an example of the drive for production and the drive towards privatization of formerly communal resources. This led to the impoverishment of landless agricultural workers and sometimes their criminalization.

As the anonymous eighteenth-century verse, 'The Goose and the Common', put it,

The law locks up the man or woman
Who steals the goose from off the common
But leaves the greater villain loose
Who steals the common from the goose.

The commons were previously shared and managed cooperatively in such a way that they wouldn't be depleted. They were managed by the boundaries of negotiated limits on what one person could take and similarly never overgrazed by local agreement. The commons being enclosed as well as stealing land from local villagers also broke down ancient structures of community ownership.

A similar land grab has been happening since the 1970s on the West Bank where Israeli settlers in contravention of international law, but feeling they have a biblical mandate, have been appropriating land from Palestinian farmers. In 2010, as part of a World Council of Churches programme, I spent three months living in the Palestinian village of Jayous and saw the cost to a formerly wealthy agricultural village of having its land annexed. Abu Assam, from one of the leading families in the village, took me up to a hill overlooking the village's former land – some of which was his. As I looked down, I could see haphazard rows of ancient olive trees stretching down the hill, then cleared land and the straight lines of two eight-foot-high electric fences bordering a dirt track which military vehicles drove along. Behind it were more olives and polytunnels owned by villagers and beyond that were the red tiles and whitewashed walls of the settlement of

Zufim, built on the village's former land. For the villagers of Jayous to get to their land beyond what they called 'The Wall' they had to have a permit and go through a checkpoint between 7 and 8.30am each morning, returning by 3pm. The six former village wells were owned by an Israeli water company from which they now had to buy water. I'd told Abu Assam that I lived on a farm and he said to me,

> Imagine having to have a permit and queue up at a checkpoint with a gun pointed at you to get to your land; imagine too not being able to sell your crops because the military had sealed off your village for days at a time. You know we call this fence the Apartheid Wall because it makes us second-class citizens.

The separation barrier that runs for nearly 400 miles, protecting Israeli settlements like Zufim, does become an eight-metre-high wall in towns like Bethlehem.

Later on the same day we're walking through the olive groves on the village side of the fence and I'm a little puzzled by the lack of boundaries on any of the land, so I ask Abu Assam, 'Why are there no fences or walls here to mark out whose property it is and how do you know which is your land and your neighbour's?' He tells me that they all know their land intimately and it has been passed down through the generations. The way they work the land is done corporately with neighbours and relations working in turn on each other's plots. 'So you see, we know very well whose land is which, we're bound by relationships and not laws and fences. The Israelis say the land belongs to us, but we say we belong to the land.'

I'm immediately reminded of how the commons used to be managed and begin to see the subtle boundaries of a more communal way of doing things compared to the cold hard borders imposed by more individualistic structures. This makes me think of the contrast between a living hedge supporting multiple systems of life and a cold metal wire fence or stone wall. The contrast between a living interrelated boundary and a dead barrier. Well-developed community bonds allow for some elasticity in boundaries and give a sense of common endeavour and belonging. Good community bonds can allow people to manage inevitable conflicts well, and prevent polarization and the shutting down of communication.

To those living on settlements, security and ownership comes through fences and the power of the military, but for the Palestinians I met, security comes through a network of relationships. I'm so attracted to this idea that we belong to the land and one another and that should be our starting point. It's how we do relationships that we should build boundaries around, not physical spaces. Relationship with one another and relationship with the earth.

This idea of being part of the land rather than owning it is there in the most sustainable cultures of our world. Indigenous people don't concentrate on physical boundaries but rather set limits on how much you take from the earth.

Boundaries are expressed most effectively not through signs explaining ownership and telling trespassers they will be prosecuted, but rather in concretely living out strong values and, guided by these, continually negotiating the difficulties of daily life.

Ritual celebrations and rites of passage can help express these values, with a sense of reverence for the earth and of kinship rather than a desire to own and control. At Pilsdon we had a ritual for passing on the responsibility of the leadership of the community, and like all good rituals nobody could remember where it had come from, only that it had been going on for years. It was the giving of the drain rods to the new warden of the community. A bundle of 15 strong but flexible black plastic rods with interlocking male and female ends would be passed on as a sign that Pilsdon expected humble and practical leadership. The ceremony always provoked humour yet also expressed the expectation that the role being taken on would be demanding, that sometimes you'd metaphorically beat people with a big stick, that it would involve hard physical work. It was a reminder that you'd get dirty and on a psychological level you'd be working in some dark and difficult places, yet there was potential for much unblocking, and when the pipe was clear, community life would flow well.

Boundaries, I'm increasingly coming to understand, are more than just borders or legal structures – all of which are necessary but too often are used to enforce control, block and assert the dominance of wealth and power. It's the unseen boundaries limiting destructive behaviour and providing structure to our common life that we need to optimise. If we get these right, through building respectful relationships with our neighbours, then the need for ever bigger and more forbidding walls will diminish

Relational boundaries

At Pilsdon we tended to put the common good over the needs of the individual. This became clearest when we needed to exclude people from the community. When people first arrived at the community and after a few days' 'trial', if the community decided they could join us and the new guest also wished to be part of our life, I would clearly lay out the non-negotiable boundaries surrounding community life. We came to call them 'The Magnificent 7':

1 Come to all meals.
2 Be prepared to work as you are able to support community life.
3 It's a dry house so anyone under the influence of alcohol or non-prescribed drugs will be asked to leave immediately.
4 No violence or intimidation, this includes shouting.
5 If you are on prescribed medication, continue taking it unless your doctor agrees to reduce it.
6 No exclusive relationships to be formed, as our experience shows these seldom work out and disrupt our common life.
7 Don't go away for the first three months.

Generally, people abided by these rules and were glad of them, particularly those struggling with addiction who needed to know that we had a clear culture of sobriety and zero tolerance towards any substance misuse. Expecting people to come to meals and work helped those struggling with poor mental health, as it meant people had to get up in the morning and establish healthy routines. If the chickens need you to let them out, it gets you up and gives the new day a sense of purpose. Everybody who joined the community was given some responsibility, however small, and all this gave direction to some who'd been without routine for years.

When people crossed the line, and it was usually around the consumption of alcohol or drugs, the community had to enforce its will. On one occasion we asked six men who we strongly suspected of smoking cannabis to leave on the same day.

Two of the most vulnerable and easily led of the rule breakers we arranged to stay at nearby Hilfield Friary for a week to consider whether they wanted to return for a second chance. Two others we found places for at a dry house in the next town and the two who had done the supplying and who we knew to be streetwise we simply dropped off in Bridport to fend for themselves. There was a huge sense of relief in the community after this radical clear-out of people. It reinforced the boundaries of the community, which in turn allowed people to feel safe. Benedict understood this when he wrote of the need for exclusion from community after frequent warnings: 'Yet even if this procedure does not heal him the Abbott must turn to the knife for amputation, following the guidance of St Paul, who told the Corinthians to banish evil from their midst.'[6]

There is an apocryphal Benedictine story that I've always liked, which says that if a guest is difficult and refuses to leave, two stout Brothers should be sent to explain things to him, and gently but firmly remove him from the monastery. Whenever we did need to exclude someone, we always did it with great respect and the hope that people might return to Pilsdon at another time. Just occasionally we'd need to call the police to remove someone. I seldom felt guilty about excluding someone as I knew it was to protect the community as a whole.

Sharing common values

Communities are threatened and sometimes destroyed when structures become lax, or members of the community begin to disrupt the common life. Key to the success of community life is the desire for people to bind themselves to the shared principles and participate fully in community life. When people applied to join Pilsdon Community, I increasingly began to look not for their gifts or skills but rather how much they wanted to be in the community. We had potential guests who had all the necessary skills to live in community, all the advantages of education, but if it was their parents not them pushing them to live in community it was unlikely to work. In contrast, I've seen men come directly from the street with ten years of chaotic life behind them, but with such a strong desire to engage and be held by community life that they've thrived against the odds.

Pilsdon had a careful policy for inviting people to come and live with us. Each guest would need to fill in an application form, provide two referees and a letter from the doctor outlining any medical conditions. The only two things that would immediately rule anyone out of coming to Pilsdon were a conviction for arson or a sexual offence committed against children or vulnerable adults. The one time we let someone in with a history of arson they attempted to set the main manor house on fire, starting fires in three different areas. She'd been an ordained priest and was thought to be low risk. It reminded us of why we set limits on who could come.

If people got through our screening process they'd be invited for a trial week, so they and the community could discern whether things might work out for them. Always we'd be looking to see their motivation for joining in and their understanding of the ethos of community life. There were times in the life of Pilsdon when the community felt strong and well resourced and at those times we were more willing to accept guests who might be more of a risk or exhibited some challenging behaviour. When our community life felt strong it meant we could take more risks with who we invited to live with us, for as a community we were able to hold more difficulty. Brother Sam, a former guardian at

Hilfield used to say that the test of a healthy community is seen in how well it responds to difficult visitors.

For potential community members at Pilsdon the same process happened but there were further levels of discernment and one or two visits before a trial fortnight and then a probationary period of six months. Finding the right people to live as community members, who would hold the vision and values of Pilsdon, live them with real intention and be able to enforce and themselves uphold the 'rule' of our common life was an important task. I liked what Roy Searle, a founder of the Northumbria Community, said to us once: 'Pray that God sends you the right people but pray even harder he keeps the wrong people away!' He was echoing Benedict's advice on the procedure for accepting new Brothers:

> Do not grant newcomers to the monastic life easy entry, but, as the Apostle says, *I test the spirits to see if they are from God* (1 John 4:1). Therefore, if someone comes and keeps knocking at the door, and if at the end of four or five days he has shown himself patient in bearing his harsh treatment and difficulty of entry, and has persisted in his request, then he should be allowed to enter and stay in the guest quarters for a few days. After that, he should live in the novitiate, where the novices study, eat and sleep.[7]

For Benedict, obedience to the rule was all important as obedience to it was what would bring life to the individual and whole community. Of the three vows a Benedictine monk takes – obedience, stability and conversion – obedience to the rule is always placed foremost. All the Franciscan Brothers I have spoken to about their vows of poverty, chastity and obedience tell me that obedience is the hardest one to live out, but often the most life-giving. My own desire to be obedient to the common life at both Pilsdon and Hilfield has sometimes been a struggle, but when I submit to the community's needs over my own, I'm grateful for the peace it brings me. Sue Langdon, a former warden of Pilsdon, remarks that when people first join the community and are chafing under some of the restrictions of life, she says to them, 'If you put Pilsdon rather than yourself first, things will work out for you.'

In his book *The City is My Monastery*, Richard Carter, founder of the Nazareth Community, a dispersed community, echoes Sue's words: 'Obedience is about creating the very conditions in which each member of the community may flourish. What at first may seem a loss is in fact the soil that allows me to flourish.'[8] Communities are held together ultimately not by the rule of law, significant though this is, but rather by shared values and common understandings that create healthy boundaries.

Living simply and sustainably

The world's longest-lasting cultures aren't those with written constitutions and complicated legal systems to protect property, but rather those with oral traditions and rituals that bind the community together in subtle, more powerful ways. Central to these largely indigenous cultures is a deep respect for the earth, a sense of our dependence on it and the interdependence of all peoples.

For 50,000 generations, human beings lived as nomadic people with a strong sense of dependence on the natural environment. It's only been in the last 500 generations that people have become settled. If you no longer move around to grow food, then it can subtly change your view of the world and your values. If you can store food as well as providing security for the winter and hard times it can also lead to a philosophy of accumulation, greed and the fear of losing wealth. Seeing wealth in the natural world no longer as a gift for all people, but rather something we gain by working hard, something that belongs to me as an individual, has led to the breakdown of numerous societies based on the pursuit of wealth secured by force. Think of the numerous empires that have grown mighty and then disintegrated. A more sustainable society is built on what we hold in common as humans and our more-than-human brothers and sisters, and it is there for us to see in more sustainable indigenous cultures.

One of the great advantages of living at Hilfield has been the lack of daily concern about what I will eat each day, where it comes from, is it ethically produced, is it local, organic? I know all this will have been dealt with by the person who orders our food, because we have adopted the 'LOAF' principles – locally grown, organic, animal friendly and fairly traded. The rules of our common life mean I can trust that what I'm eating is bound by our shared values. Every year in May at Rogationtide (*rogare* being the Latin for 'to ask'), we 'beat the bounds' of the community land and buildings asking for God's blessing on the natural world and all that sustains us. One of the community priests will joyously splash holy water on our fields, sheep, chickens, cattle, pigs, the new seedlings in the vegetable garden, the woodland, the log pile, the workshop, our borehole, the kitchen and all the sources of our common life. It takes a good hour, and we always end under the gospel oak, a 500-plus-year-old tree on the edge of our land. Under its newly leafed boughs is a good place to gather for a final prayer praying for and acknowledging God's blessing on the land and reminding us of our dependence on it.

Being held by the annual cycles

The keeping of the church year is central to the life of the friary and brings a shape and richness to our life together and binds us together in oft-repeated rituals. Beginning in late November or early December, the season of Advent marks a time of waiting, not knowing, looking at the darkness of our world and some of our own shadows. The chapel is kept bare of adornment. Not a single carol is sung before Midnight Mass, which ushers in the 12 days of Christmas, a joyous time of hospitality and feasting, with the chapel beams covered in so much greenery it feels like entering a forest save for the flickering light of candles everywhere. Then it's Epiphany, with the statues of magi adding a sense of eastern mysticism and the Scripture readings urging us to look for signs of glory and God's revelation in the world. Then Candlemas with its bittersweet themes of birth and death standing between Christmas and Holy Week. Then the season of Lent with its theme of penitence and again all decoration is removed from the chapel. Then we move into the drama of Holy Week, beginning with a procession from the camping field commemorating Jesus' triumphal entry into Jerusalem with us waving not palms but pussy willow just coming into bloom. Then the washing of feet on Maundy Thursday reminding us of Christ's call to humility, and the commemoration of Jesus' Last Supper, the total stripping of the chapel. A procession then leads people to a re-creation of the Garden of Gethsemane and a rota of community members take turns in watching and praying until daylight. From the Thursday, evening bells are no longer rung; instead, a 1950s football rattle summons people to sombre meals. On Good Friday, a giant battered wooden cross is laid on the chapel floor and the Passion Gospel is read dramatically. Then the cross is carried around the friary where community members and guests offer reflections, some visual, some sung, some mimed out on the theme of crucifixion in our world and of our planet. Holy Saturday follows as a quiet day pondering death and our own mortality and what it means to live in liminal time.

Easter morning begins in the dark with a giant bonfire in the community burial ground, where the Easter candle is lit and processed into the chapel, then a whole series of readings from the Old and New Testaments chart God's liberating work, culminating in the reading of the Easter Gospel. Then every bell in the friary is rung and we process into the courtyard, singing, and bottles of fizzy wine and our own apple juice are opened and served with home-made biscuits. The ritual of the whole week seems to come alive as we exit the church to the sound of bells and the spring light; our belief that through the life and death and resurrection of Jesus Christ death is somehow overcome is held by the ancient and sometimes new customs we follow.

Forty days after Easter, following Morning Prayer, we climb onto a flat roof three storeys above the ground and sing 'Hail the Day that sees Him Rise', as the swallows and house martins fly around us. Then comes Pentecost when we give thanks for the gift of the Holy Spirit, opening the church up to all nations, followed by Trinity Sunday stressing the social nature of God. On 11 August we celebrate St Clare's day, followed in October by

St Francis. And then we begin again. To be held in these ancient patterns somehow feels reassuring and of course accompanies the cycle of the seasons.

Keeping healthy boundaries with one another

As well as corporate traditions, which give shape to the year and each day, for a community to function well individuals need to learn to keep healthy boundaries with each other and how they balance work, leisure, study, time off and time with family and friends. The art of living well in community is about allowing yourself to find a balance between the many demands and opportunities of community life. Some members at Hilfield are naturally gregarious and energized by communal meals and regular visitors. Others more towards the introvert end of the spectrum need to learn to build solitude into their day, so as not to be overwhelmed by the sheer volume of conversations you can have each day. Those of us who are always keen to help have to learn not to volunteer for everything.

While being obedient to the life of the community, each individual has to find sustainable ways to live within their limits so as not to be crushed by what can sometimes seem the endless demands of the community. Unlike the traditional work environment, community life doesn't end at 5pm each day or for the weekend. So each member of the community needs to set their own boundaries. Adam, a former community leader at Pilsdon, always used to have a 20-minute nap after lunch, which got him through the rest of the afternoon, and everyone knew not to disturb him then. At Pilsdon, such was the anxiety of some of the guests, and such was their need to unburden themselves, that if you didn't set limits on the time you spent with them, you could quickly become exhausted by the weight of their pain and suffering. I quickly came to learn that I wasn't at Pilsdon to help 'fix' people, but rather to be part of a community that held people really well, in a way that could allow people to experience healing. I learnt to trust in the structures and rhythms of Pilsdon to do their work. If people needed counselling or other forms of therapeutic support, this was always provided by services outside the community. My front door was a boundary I never let anyone cross, to clearly delineate between my down time at home and community life. If someone came to the door in crisis, I would always take them down to a community room or see them outside. Once there was a man so anxious that he followed me into the toilet to talk to me. I had to gently explain to him where we were and that I'd see him in a minute!

The boundaries of appropriate touch and language are areas that demand great sensitivity and self-awareness in community life. Safeguarding policies help in this, particularly when things go badly wrong, but real care needs to be taken with each individual in community. We all have different comfort zones when it comes to physical proximity and the amount we wish to share with each other.

I was on a panel talking about community at the Greenbelt Festival. A question came to the panel: 'What about people having sex in community and falling in love with each other, I've seen it destroy several communities?' The three other panellists turned and looked at me with the same panic in their eyes that I felt, so I framed an answer. I said in a deadpan voice,

> Sex happens. And of course how communities respond to new exclusive relationships depends on each community. At Pilsdon, because of the vulnerabilities of so many of our guests, we tended to discourage intimate and exclusive relationships, but accepted that they would happen and when they did we would encourage one or both of the new couple to leave. In contrast, at the more stable Hilfield Friary when two of the volunteers came to Brother Sam to tell him that one of them was pregnant, his reply was, 'O good the Community is going to have a baby!' It seems to me the main thing is to deal with each situation with compassion and care and to try and discern whether it is a threat to or an opportunity for community life.

The boundaries parents in community keep around the upbringing of their children depend on the needs of each family and are probably worthy of a book in their own right.

The discipline of taking days off and holidays and retreats over the years has been a huge help in keeping up my enthusiasm for community life. At Hilfield, our Sabbath runs from Sunday after lunch when our guests leave until Tuesday morning when new weekly guests arrive. It allows us a break from the constant demand to be attentive to a wide range of visitors and by Tuesday lunchtime we are refreshed and ready for new arrivals.

A balance to community life can be helped by the assignment of roles and tasks in the community and finding the right person for key roles. Benedict lays particular emphasis on finding the right person to be the community leader or abbot: 'Goodness of life and wisdom in teaching must be the criteria of choosing one to be abbot, even if he is last in community rank.'[9] He goes on to say that if a community elects the wrong person who leads them in 'evil ways' it's up to the local bishop or other abbots in the area to see he is removed. Chapter 31, entitled 'Qualification for the Cellarer', suggests that the person responsible for distributing the food and drink should be, 'Someone who is wise, mature in conduct, temperate, not an excessive eater, not proud, excitable, dilatory or wasteful, but God fearing and like a father to the whole community.'[10] At Pilsdon, we found that giving our guests roles and responsibilities allowed people to grow in confidence and a sense of belonging. So people would become the 'Pilsdon Shepherd', 'The Pilsdon Swineherd', the 'Laundry Tsar' and so on.

Central to the smooth running of Pilsdon and to Hilfield too is a series of rotas. Pilsdon had a chapel rota, cooking rota, milking rota, dairy rota, floor-washing rota and a fire list to be updated daily as new guests and wayfarers arrived. The rotas make sure work gets done and is shared out fairly, and people are drawn into community life and provide a framework for each day and week. What the lists can't do is make sure the work is done willingly and without the grumbling and resentment that can erode community life. At Pilsdon, there was inevitably a lot of moaning about people not pulling their weight with work and ironically it was the people who were the tardiest in terms of work who seemed to complain most. My reply to them was that I loved the work and did it to my best and didn't want to waste my energy on worrying about other people. When I did lapse into resenting those less enthusiastic about community life, it was a sure sign that I was getting overtired and had given in to the temptation to do too many of the things I loved and maybe I needed to ask for help. In community, some need to be encouraged to do more but some less. That's where a community rule of life can be so helpful. In the prologue to his rule, Benedict writes, 'In drawing up its regulations, we hope to set down nothing harsh, nothing burdensome. The good of all concerned, however, may prompt us to a little strictness in order to amend faults and to safeguard love.'[11]

For friars in the Society of St Francis, the equivalent of Benedict's rule is found in their Principles of the First Order, sections of which are read each day after Morning Prayer. Lay members of the Third Order of the Society of St Francis are encouraged to adopt their own Rule of Life, which is reviewed each year. It covers commitments to daily prayer, living simply, working for peace and justice and seeking to follow in the way of St Francis. Adopting a rule of life is something that anyone can do in order to help boundary and direct their life in a more dynamic and intentional way. Typically, a rule of life might centre on creating a daily structure for prayer, contemplation, manual work, creativity, exercise, study, perhaps a weekly form of the same including a day off for Sabbath, annual times of retreat, holidays. For those already belonging to a faith community it can help us work out how to live well within the discipline of that community.

When healthy patterns and rhythms are internalized and given expression in considered ways then our communities are strengthened. Rules for living that keep us attentive to the needs of other people and the living communities of the natural are what make life both joyful and sustainable.

Rules of course can only take you so far and it's the interpretation and living out of them that is crucial, and perhaps the virtue that helps us most with this is humility.

Questions

1 Where in the Old Testament do we find evidence of boundaries?

2 What is Jesus' approach to boundaries?

3 How are limits and patterns in your life helpful?

4 How easy is it for you to negotiate boundaries with others?

5 How do we as a nation balance keeping safe borders with the call to be hospitable to those in danger?

Practical suggestions

1 Read the rule of St Benedict or the Quakers' *Advices and queries*, both quite short.

2 If you don't have one consider adopting a 'Rule of Life'.

3 Make sure you take good time off and each week contains a Sabbath.

4 Try and ensure each day has a balance of work and play, conviviality and solitude and time outdoors.

Notes

1 Timothy Fry (trans.), 1982, *The Rule of St Benedict*, Collegeville, MN: Liturgical Press, p. 18.

2 Michael Northcott, 2015, *Place, Ecology and the Sacred*, London: Bloomsbury, p. 47.

3 Fry, *The Rule of St Benedict*, p. 9.

4 Tim Adams, 2023, 'Every river in this country is polluted': how Feargal Sharkey got swept up by the clean water campaign', *The Guardian*, 9 April, https://www.theguardian.com/environment/2023/apr/09/every-river-in-this-country-is-polluted-how-feargal-sharkey-got-swept-up-by-the-clean-water-campaign, accessed 19.01.2026.

5 Walter Brueggemann, 2014, *Sabbath as Resistance*, Louisville, KY: Westminster John Knox Press, p. 85.

6 Fry, *The Rule of St Benedict*, p. 28.

7 Fry, *The Rule of St Benedict*, p. 78

8 Richard Carter, 2019, *The City is My Monastery*, London: Canterbury Press, p. 167.

9 Fry, *The Rule of St Benedict*, p. 87.

10 Fry, *The Rule of St Benedict*, p. 54.

11 Fry, *The Rule of St Benedict*, p 19.

4

Humility

I'm sitting in the latest model of the Toyota Landcruiser, grateful for its air conditioning as we wait to board the ferry to cross the River Gambia from south to north. Ahead of us is a haphazard queue of lorries full of sacks of rice, groundnuts, millet and branches of green bananas and plantain, becalmed taxis with brightly clad passengers standing outside smoking and waiting to move forward. Their patience is in contrast to my friend, the Right Reverend Tilewa Johnson, the Bishop of the Gambia, who I am visiting to chaplain the gathering of the churches in his diocese. He's a huge man, six foot five, a powerfully built former basketball player for the national team, and he's starting to get frustrated. He lowers his window and calls one of the ferry operators over and demands to go to the front of the queue; he tells the man who, from his white cap and full beard, is obviously from Gambia's 95 per cent Muslim population, that he is a senior religious leader like an Imam and needs to be treated as such. The man smiles, shakes his head and walks away. Infuriated, Tilewa gets on the phone to his Lebanese friend from the old colonial club where he plays tennis, who owns the ferry company. Within five minutes we are at the front of the queue and driving onto the boat and soon across the river.

I'm feeling embarrassed by this pulling the strings of privilege but, as a guest and the only white man for miles around, I say nothing as we power through the darkening night along a Chinese-built road to our destination at the Diocesan Centre at Farafenni on the southern edge of the Sahara. We arrive about 10pm only to find the gates to the compound shut. The bishop is furious as he expects people to be waiting to greet him, not to be locked out. 'But, Bishop,' I say, 'didn't you tell me that the compound was in decline and all the fences round it falling down. If we drive round the edge I'm sure we can get in.' Sure enough a gap in the fence appears and we drive over the sandy soil and arrive at a grass-thatched round building, which is the chapel. The bishop tries to enter it to give thanks for our safe arrival, but finds it locked. 'Send for the priest!' he bellows. 'The bishop wants to pray in the chapel.' Quickly, the bleary-eyed priest arrives in shorts and a T-shirt. 'Open the chapel,' the bishop demands.

'But I don't have the key,' says the priest.

'But you're the priest, who has the keys?' the bishop rages.

'Mr Ouja the headteacher has the keys, Bishop.'

'Then send for Mr Ouja!'

Mr Ouja arrives and starts to unlock the door, but the bishop stops him. He takes the keys, and says, 'You are the priest, take these keys as a sign of your authority and now open the door.' We enter calmly but for a final time the bishop's anger pours forth, 'Look at the state of this chapel! I want it painted before I come back here in the morning. Now let us pray.'

For the next three days, Bishop Tilewa leads the conference, with great energy, humour and authority. The gathering is to end with a service followed by a feast. The service includes baptisms, confirmation, the ordination of three deacons, the formal closing of synod, and lasts nearly four hours. I've been asked to preach, and told that I'm expected to speak for a minimum of 45 minutes, which is in contrast to my usual speaking engagements when there's a maximum of 15 minutes. As we are ordaining deacons, I choose to preach on serving others and the gift of humility.

I remind the congregation of Christ's call to renounce power, how he enters Jerusalem on a donkey, a humble beast of burden in a parody of a Roman imperial procession. How he tells his followers 'unless a grain of wheat falls and dies it remains a single grain', reminding his followers that the son of man came not to be served but to serve, how he tells us that those who are exalted will be humbled and the humble raised up in God's kingdom. I've got 45 minutes so I keep banging on about humility and my visual aid is a towel as I retell the story of Jesus washing his disciples' feet as their servant. Finally, the service ends and the feast begins. The bishop takes off his robes and with great energy begins to organize the queues in his rolled-up shirt sleeves, waving his arms rather like an old-fashioned traffic policeman. First, the newly ordained deacons and their families are fed, then the newly baptized and confirmed and their families, then the members of synod and then the 300 or so people from the nearby villages, the bishop making sure the children go first. The last person to eat is the bishop. I take him over a beer from a bucket with huge lumps of melting ice in it, sit down next to him and with a huge grin he says to me, 'I listened to your sermon you know!'

Humility is at the heart of living well together and a foundational Christian virtue. Each day following Morning Prayer the Principles of the First Order of the Society of St Francis are read in the chapel at Hilfield Friary and I'm always struck by the reading for Day 25 on humility:

> Humility is the recognition of the truth about God and ourselves, the recognition of our own insufficiency and dependence, seeing that we have nothing which we have not received. It is the mother of all Christian virtues, as St Bernard of Clairvaux has said. No spiritual house can stand for a moment save on the foundation of humility.[1]

The people who've been my best mentors in community are the people who quietly get on with life, doing many of the unseen and often dirty jobs, embodying a silent hidden heroism. At Hilfield, our bell ringer, Keith, always emptied people's bins, took the rubbish bag from the kitchen each night and dragged out the recycling bins every Tuesday night. Brother Hugh looks after our sewage works and has the even smellier job of cleaning the fat trap. I'm the chief unblocker of drains, though that's usually a more public and dramatic role as I only ever do it when it becomes a problem. Uriel uncomplainingly makes countless trips back and forth with the tractor loading our biomass boiler with woodchip. At Pilsdon, Henry was the person who silently appeared to help with the disposal of a dead animal or barrow three straw bales into the vegetable garden at 9pm on a May evening to save the potatoes from an unexpected frost. Henry is an early riser so, before anyone else is even up, fresh bread mysteriously appears. If I was in the kitchen in either community Hugh or Henry would often appear – silently in Henry's case, and more noisily in Hugh's – and clear a mound of washing up, before disappearing again. St Francis was reputed to have said, 'Go out into the world and proclaim the gospel and use words only if you have to.'

The people who are less helpful in community are the ones who in contrast bring up little complaints about uncompleted tasks or point out the jobs that need doing without offering their help, instead strictly sticking to their allotted jobs on the rota. It's not the bigger, more public expressions of community life that cement life together – important as they are – but the small, often hidden things, quietly got on with, that help us grow together.

The humility of the Little Sisters and Brothers of Jesus

This sense of the importance of the hidden and the ordinary is seen in the spirituality of Charles de Foucauld and the ongoing witness of the Little Sisters and Little Brothers of Jesus. Charles was born in 1858 in France into an aristocratic family and became a cavalry officer. In the army he led a life of indolence, describing himself as sleeping long, eating much and thinking little. He left the army to become an explorer and his experience of being alone in the Sahara Desert began to change him. On return to Paris, he rediscovered his Catholic faith and entered the silence of a Trappist monastery. He loved the simplicity of monastic life but felt called to live even more simply like Jesus as a poor workman of Nazareth. Taken on as a servant by the community of the Poor Clares in Nazareth, he wrote the Rule of the Little Brothers. His rule emphasized the 30 unseen, hidden years of Jesus' life in Nazareth. He returned to Paris where he was ordained priest and then went to Algeria to set up a monastery. Nobody joined him, due to the administrative difficulties of Europeans entering Algeria and perhaps the austerity of his life.

He died in 1916 after living ten years among the Tuareg people, killed in the political upheavals brought on by World War One.

Above all, his way of living stressed humility. Quoting Luke's Gospel, he said,

> 'he went down with them and came to Nazareth and was subject to them' (Luke 2.51). He went down and humbled himself – his life was one of humility. Being God you took on the appearance of man, you made yourself the least of men.[2]

His was a life of obscurity and apparent failure but in 1933, inspired by his vision and called to a community life of poverty and humility, Rene Voillaume founded the Little Brothers of Jesus and in 1939 the Little Sisters of Jesus began under the leadership of Sister Madeleine. Today there are dozens of small community houses around the world where Brothers and Sisters live in the poorest and most marginalized communities. They take jobs of manual labour or care work, living in great simplicity. I visited the Little Sisters on the thirteenth floor in a tower block in Tottenham, north London and felt blessed by the simple and joyful welcome I received. When I met Brother Ian in a rough area of Peckham, in the same street where Damilola Taylor bled to death in a stairwell after being attacked with a broken bottle in 2000, I asked him if he felt vulnerable living on the ground floor of his block of flats. 'No,' he laughed. 'No one locally would dream of robbing me, they know I have nothing; I'm protected by poverty.'

A freedom in humility

There's a joy and freedom that comes with having nothing and seeking to be humble and no longer subjugated by the demands of ego and the expectations of others. When we live from a more egotistical place there is less room for others. The more space we fill, the more we can diminish others. Humility can bind a group together, recognizing not just your own gifts but provoking gratitude for the gifts of others. Humility directly challenges the destructive narratives of competition, individualism and self-interest.

As Joan Chittister writes,

> Competition infects every dimension of society: education, business, politics, play. Nothing is done for its own sake. Everything is done to win something, to get something, to best someone else ... It's the comparative value of a person that counts in a society such as this, not the personality or the character or the morality or the simple deep-down goodness of people committed to, as St. Philippine Duchesne put it, 'simple duty daily done'.[3]

In his book *The Place of Tides* James Rebanks travels to a remote Norwegian island to join Anna, a 'duck woman' who maintains the local tradition of protecting and creating nests for eider ducks and then collecting their feathers. It's a tough and at times humiliating experience for him but ultimately transformative as Anna's simplicity and focused humble way of working contrasts with his own sense of ego-drivenness. Towards the end of his stay he realizes,

> the past few years I have been swallowed up by striving. I remember a friend back home trying to tell me gently, that I had become almost manic. But the longer I spent with Anna, the more that way of being felt like a sickness I needed to recover from. A new calmness began to settle over me. It was a feeling I had not known since I was a child following my grandfather round the fields.[4]

His experience of extended retreat leads Rebanks to the conclusion that it is the hidden humble work of conservation embodied in the life of Anna that is both personally transformative and what builds up human communities and leads to the protection of our ecosystems:

> We have to show up day in day out for years and years doing the work. There will be no brass band, no parade. And we have

> to accept and keep the faith in each other and somehow work together. It is the only way we can make our own tiny deeds add up to become the change we need.[5]

Rebanks, echoing Gandhi's words – 'be the change you need' – confirms my experience of community life, that change comes slowly and often through the repetition of mundane tasks done individually and for the common good.

Awe at nature humbles us

What helped him come to this place of humility, along with the example of Anna, was a sense of awe and sometimes fear at the power of the North Sea and the changing tides and seasons. Contact with nature and particular places of wilderness can help us move from a place where human beings and self are at the centre of our world to realize that we are just a small part of a complex and beautiful web of intimately connected relationships. The word 'humanity' has the same root as 'humus', the thin layer of soil on which we depend for our food supply. In the biblical creation story, Adam is formed from the earth and Jesus' favourite way to describe himself is as the son of man or Adamah – literally earth man. If you were to pick up a handful of dark well-rotted soil from the Hilfield compost bin you'd be holding over ten billion living organisms; that's rich soil. Schleiermacher famously said humanity would do well to contemplate the vastness of creation by either looking through a telescope at the cosmos or a microscope to see the complexity of life. 'When I look at your heavens, the work of your fingers, the moon and the stars that you have established; what are human beings that you are mindful of them?', says the Psalmist (Ps. 8.3–4).

Awe can lead to a humbling, but also a sense of deep connection to 'the more-than-human world'. During the 2020 lockdown and during Lent, every Wednesday afternoon a group of us from Hilfield went to pray under the shadow of a great oak tree on the edge of our woodland. The oak probably planted itself when England was still a Catholic country, survived the Civil War, two world wars and is continuing to grow. It was humbling to sit under such a venerable tree and each week as spring came in to see it come into leaf and notice its slow constant aliveness. A mature oak can support over 2,000 species, and looking up into its mighty boughs I began to feel quite small and finite. Lynne from the community said, 'I began going out each week to pray for a restoration of nature and for the climate emergency and then began to realize that the tree was praying for me.' It's that sort of conversion that puts us in our proper place. When we begin to live from a place of profound connection with, and gratitude for, nature, rather than the still-prevailing domination narrative that nature is a commodity to be used for our benefit, we will begin to understand the need for relationships that bind and sustain us. I wonder if we need to hear once more like Job the voice of God from the whirlwind: 'Where were you when I laid the foundation of the earth? Tell me, if you have understanding' (Job 38.4) and, like Job, repent in dust and ashes.

In *The Living Mountain* Nan Shepherd writes about her lifetime of walking in the Cairngorms and reflects something of her sense of smallness compared with the immensity of the plateau, the rocks, the light, flowing water. She speaks of how walkers and climbers wish to conquer the mountain and reach its highest points, but for her she almost walks into the mountain, rejoicing in its recesses and repeated relationship with it over the years:

> Yet even the mountain gives itself most completely when I have no destination, when I reach nowhere in particular, but have gone out merely to be with the mountain as one visits a friend with no intention but to be with him.[6]

Her deep sense of belonging to and losing herself in something bigger than herself is in such contrast to our consumer-driven culture that drives people to seek to possess and control rather than be part of something bigger. The hubris that is destroying so much of nature and leading to a planet that will be too hot for humans safely to inhabit has at its heart a separation of ourselves from and an objectification of nature, which then allows us to seek to dominate it. In contrast to this narrative of separation is the story of community, which accepts our weaknesses and vulnerabilities and dependence on one another. Every healthy ecosystem is made up of a complex network of interdependencies. Recent tree science is beginning to show us the existence of a complex system of mycorrhizal fungi underground that allow tree roots to access and convert nutrients from the ground. Our mighty gospel oak is dependent for its survival on tiny microscopic organisms hidden below the humus.

Living in community is, for me, increasingly becoming more than just living with my human brothers and sisters, but also developing a deep sense of kinship with the landscape, the trees, the soil, the watercourses, the birds, the insects and the animals that we share our land with. Delighting in the first swallow to return, the hoot of the tawny owl, the deepening colours of the autumn trees, and the winter stars, reminds me how small I am but also how I belong as a son of the earth.

Non-violence

Sitting, kneeling or walking gently on the ground has been a way of my becoming aware of my dependence on the earth, but also a sign of my resistance to structures of power that seek to dominate and control creation. In September 2020, myself and the Revd Hilary Bond decided to hold a prayer vigil throughout the night on the grass of Parliament Square, opposite the building where the Climate and Nature Bill was due to be debated the next day. The police had cleared the square with a Section 14 Order, but we decided to stay until we were arrested. We knelt on prayer stools, eyes shut as the police began to debate what to do, and then we were joined by the Revd Sue Parfitt, who proceeded to celebrate a simple Eucharist with the police watching on. As she finished, they asked us to leave or we would be arrested, but we stayed silent. They said again, 'Do you understand if you don't move we will arrest you?' We silently nodded. I returned to the mantra I was silently repeating and waited. Nothing happened and they moved away. We waited quietly, not knowing what would happen next. At midnight with the change of shift the new inspector came to see us and said they'd decided not to arrest us, but they might still do so. We then prayed the ancient prayers of compline, the words flickering up from our phones, 'My soul waits for the Lord, more than those who watch for the morning' (Ps. 130.6). We waited, we sat on the ground, slowly and prayerfully walked around the square under the shadow of the great plane trees there and waited. Slowly the light changed and the darkness slowly and subtly formed into morning replacing the street lights. I felt humbled that even in one of the great cities of the world the dawn was still beautiful to behold.

Tea was brought to us and at 8am with the sun shining down on us from above Parliament, the first protestor, appropriately called Blaze, arrived to end our vigil.

Virtually all the protests and actions I've been on have involved sitting on the ground, kneeling or walking slowly and mindfully. There's an intentional humility in such postures as they symbolize our desire to act non-violently. If you're sitting on the ground, you're placing yourself in a defenceless position, even more so if you've glued yourself to the pavement. Common to all the actions of Christian Climate Action, Insulate Britain and Just Stop Oil was the requirement that all participants underwent non-violence training.

Non-violence is much more than a technique or a tool; more a way of living that rejects both violence and passivity in the face of oppression. It seeks to point to a new way of living together with humility at its heart. Gandhi's teaching on non-violence drew from the Hindu principle of *ahimsa*, or not harming other living beings, which is also part of Jain and Buddhist philosophy, but his thought was also much influenced by Jesus' teaching from the Sermon on the Mount. When I've been on disruptive Insulate Britain and Just Stop Oil protests it has often felt like stepping into the Beatitudes: 'Blessed are the poor in spirit ... blessed are the meek ... blessed are those who hunger and thirst for righteousness ... blessed are you when people revile you and persecute you' (Matt. 5.3–11). Never in the last six years of civil disobedience from those in the climate movement have I seen or heard reported any acts of violence against the police or anyone else – often in the face of extreme provocation. The discipline of activists has been remarkable and reveals how a commitment to act humbly is a necessary path towards peace and justice and is also a way of binding a community together. Charismatic leaders, powered by ego, come and go but a commitment to shared principles learnt through symbolic action will last a lifetime and beyond.

Living humbly and peaceably

Taking the knee became popular with Premier League footballers in 2020 following the killing of George Floyd and the emergence of 'Black Lives Matter', but its history went beyond Colin Kaepernick's protest against racism in 2016 during Donald Trump's first term as President of the United States. It went back to Martin Luther King kneeling in prayer before the march in Selma in 1965, and prior to that the image of a black slave kneeling in chains with the quotation, 'Am I not a man and a brother?' on pottery produced by Josiah Wedgewood to encourage the abolitionist movement. It has its roots in Paul's letter to the Philippians 2.5–11, which stresses the humility of Christ which leads to his suffering and death but ends with the assertion that Christ is the one before whom 'every knee should bend' (Phil. 2.10).

Violence separates people but non-violence is what builds up the beloved community, and listening to one another well is part of this process. In Christian Climate Action each meeting will often begin with a 'check in' – a time people can share and be listened to without judgement or comment. I always find meetings go much better, particularly online, if we begin with recognizing the value of each person. Too often meetings get straight down to business and can be dominated by the loudest and most assertive. My favourite way to start a meeting is with a few minutes of shared silence and I usually find these meetings are the most productive. Something that the Quakers continue to witness to in their Sunday meetings.

Non-violent communication, as pioneered by Marshall Rosenberg, is a way of improving relationships in community, by helping us to recognize the needs and feelings each of us has and to honestly communicate them. This is in contrast to more aggressive, judgemental and demanding communication that can lead to misunderstanding and fractured relationships that so often is the predominant model of discourse. Non-violent communication is about identifying the feelings and needs that are lurking below the surface and humbly and openly acknowledging them to others. When people are willing to speak from a place of vulnerability and authenticity, my experience is that it can free up others to share more freely and is a great way of building trust in community life.

Living from the false self

Each day at the friary is an opportunity to try and live more humbly by simply and quietly getting on with tasks, listening to others but crucially listening to my ego's desire to be noticed and celebrated. Thomas Merton described living from a place of ego and judgement as the false self:

> Every one of us is shadowed by an illusory person; a false self. My false and private self wants to exist outside the reach of God's will and God's love – outside of reality and outside of life. And such a self cannot but help be an illusion.[7]

Recognizing this false self in ourselves and seeking to live from our true selves, hidden in Christ through simple contemplative prayer that shuts out the prompting of our ego, was for Merton a radical life-giving humility. It's something my mentors in community life like Malcom, Hugh, Uriel and Henry continually teach me. It's not about trying harder to be good, but about letting go of false images of myself. My being less driven by my ego and its craving after power and recognition makes room for others in community. John the Baptist expresses this well when he says, 'He must increase, but I must decrease' (John 3.30). I try to remember this on the feast day commemorating John's birth, which falls just after the summer solstice as the days begin to shorten. It stands in contrast to Christmas, the feast of Christ's birth, which comes after the winter solstice when the days lengthen – a beautiful rhythm in creation that mirrors the call to humility and hope.

Contemplative prayer can greatly assist us in decreasing the power of our ego and increasing God's power in us. The letting go of all distractions, images and words helps us abandon our investment in our own sense of self-importance and makes room for God and others. It's amazing how doing nothing, being nothing, can help us grow in love of each other. The more we can empty ourselves of preoccupation and fear, the more we make room for others. A wonderful paradox of how me being less builds up the community.

The men and women who retreated to the Egyptian desert at the end of the third century, partly in protest at Christianity aligning itself with the Constantinian Empire, were famous for their humility of life.

> A brother in Scete happened to commit a fault, and the elders assembled, and sent for Abbot Moses to join them. He, however, did not want to come. The priest sent the Abbot a message, saying, 'Come, the community is waiting for you.' So he arose and started off. And taking with him a very old basket full of holes, he filled it with sand and carried it behind him. The elders came out to meet the Abbot and said: 'What is this, Father?' The Abbot replied: 'My sins are running out behind me, and I do not see them, and today I come to judge the sins of another!' They, hearing this, said nothing to the brother but pardoned him.[8]

It's far too easy to rush to judgement, but knowing our own weaknesses and fallibilities can help prevent this. Humility too allows us to laugh at ourselves when we recognize ourselves getting puffed up, and its end result is an infectious joy. When we live less from the false self of the ego it's much easier to accept the weaknesses of others and be more authentically ourselves and that makes us easier to live with and so contributes to the good of the whole. Humility is a key component for building trust. Charles de Foucauld's 'Prayer of Abandonment' beautifully links radical humility and total trust:

> Father, I abandon myself into your hands;
> do with me what you will.
> Whatever you may do, I thank you.
> I am ready for all, I accept all.
> Let only your will be done in me,
> and in all your creatures.
> I wish no more than this, O Lord.
> Into your hands I commend my soul;
> I offer it to you with all the love of my heart,
> for I love you, Lord, and so need to give myself,
> to surrender myself into your hands,
> without reserve,
> and with boundless confidence,
> for you are my Father.[9]

It's to this radical trust that we now turn.

Questions

1 Who in your faith tradition teaches about humility?

2 Who inspires you today by their humble living?

3 When and where have you felt great awe in the presence of the natural world?

4 Have you ever managed to humble yourself to make room for another?

5 How easy do you find forgiveness?

Practical suggestions

1 Spend a little time standing under a great oak, or on the seashore on a windy day to experience the immensity of the natural world.

2 Explore Non-Violent Communication, www.cnvc.org.

3 Consider learning by heart the 'Prayer of Abandonment' by Charles De Foucauld.

4 Keep in mind the Quaker saying, 'Think it possible that you may be mistaken'.

5 Keep noticing when your ego and desire for prestige are motivating your actions. Notice too your humble acts of service.

Notes

1 *The Daily Office SSF*, 2010, London: Mowbray, p. 800.

2 Charles de Foucauld, 1999, *Charles De Foucauld: Writings Selected with an Introduction by Robert Ellsberg*, Maryknoll, NY: Orbis Books, p. 48.

3 Joan Chittister, 2025, 'The power of humility', *The Monastic Way*, April.

4 James Rebanks, 2024, *The Place of Tides*, London: Allen Lane, p. 148.

5 Rebanks, *The Place of Tides*, p. 239.

6 Nan Shepherd, 2018, *The Living Mountain*, London: Canongate, p. 15.

7 Thomas Merton, 1962, *New Seeds of Contemplation*, London: Burns and Oates, p. 27.

8 Thomas Merton, 1974, *The Wisdom of the Desert*, London: Sheldon, p. 40.

9 Charles de Foucauld, https://charlesdefoucauld.org, accessed 22.04.2026.

5

Trust

It started with a phone call from a vicar in Poole who had a large number of settled Romany Gypsies living in his parish. He told me that a neighbourhood police officer had been in touch regarding a Gypsy family who'd had their horse impounded by bailiffs working on behalf of Poole Borough Council.

I went to visit the family the next day on a red-brick council estate, and sat with tea in the front room, amid boxing trophies, cut-glass vases and pictures of horses and waggons. As different generations of the family came and went, they told me the tale: how the horse had been taken, and how they'd managed to reclaim their horse after paying the specialized horse bailiffs £1,600. It was like they were recounting a trauma. They'd borrowed the money, as 'Jigsaw' was much loved by their severely autistic grandson, but couldn't really understand what had happened. The grandfather kept repeating, 'But Lady Wimborne allowed us to graze our horses on her land.' We walked to where the horse had been grazing on an overgrown bit of council land underneath a pylon. Attached to it I spotted a warning notice telling the owner of the horse to remove it in two days or the horse would be impounded. None of the family could read so they had ignored the plastic sheet of A4.

It was a classic case of two very different cultures meeting: an ancient oral tradition based on word of mouth, meeting a tradition based on the written word. A timeless nomadic way of thinking based on relationship and negotiation butting up against a more fixed procedural way of doing things. It was a clash between a covenantal tradition meeting a contractual one.

I promised the family I would talk to the council and see if we could prevent it happening again. It took nearly three months of increasingly more assertive emails – finally writing to the leader of the council – before I got a face-to-face meeting with a senior officer in Poole Borough Council along with a member of Kushti Bok, a Dorset Traveller-led charity. Over coffee he described the conflict between the council and local Travellers wishing to tether and graze their horses on bits of council land. Things had once got so heated that members of his staff had been threatened and a vehicle damaged. To protect his staff, a private specialized firm of horse bailiffs had been contracted to deal with what he called illegal grazing. I explained a bit of the Traveller's side, how owning a horse was, for people forced to settle in houses, a way of keeping a link to their nomadic past. I also explained that there was a strong belief that Lady Wimborne had given local Romany Gypsies the right to graze on her land and, though she had died in 1927 and some of her land had passed to the council, in an oral tradition that values folk memory, that wasn't so long ago. We agreed that the next time a problem with illegal grazing occurred, rather than call the bailiffs in, the council could call either me or Betty Smith Billington, the Chair of Kushti Bok.

Sure enough, some months later I had an anonymous call from the same council officer, saying, 'Off the record I'm calling you to let you know that we have an issue with a Gypsy horse. Could you sort it out please?' I rang one of my Romany friends in Poole who promised to find out whose horse it was and get them to move it. The problem was solved through the Council trusting me to mediate, and through relationships of trust with some Traveller families I'd built up over the years. Trust builds relationships and strengthens community.

Covenantal and contractual relationships

Rabbi Jonathan Sacks wrote about the erosion of covenantal relationships and the rise of contractual relationships. Organizations such as the family, churches or voluntary groups, where the members work for the common good and which are founded on trust, are slowly being destroyed by competition and more formal contractual relationships. The privatization and outsourcing of government contracts, as in the case of the horse bailiffs, lead to the erosion of common values. Contracts tend to be about self-interest, are often short term and are transactional in nature. Covenants are based on reciprocity, are long term and based on relationship. Covenantal relationships are based on trust, contractual relationships are based on mistrust, and the need to have things written down to keep people honest.

I don't have a contract to live at Hilfield Friary but each year on the First Sunday of Advent each community member commits themselves to another year living together, in a short one-page liturgy. I find a great freedom in committing to live just one year at a time, trying to respond collectively each day to the challenges life together throws up. It's about trust in one another, our vision and ultimately trust in God. The most contractual we get at Hilfield is the weekly rotas for cooking and leading worship in the chapel, but these can be wonderfully fluid with people falling sick or members having to respond to unplanned emergencies and always someone steps in to cover. Trust is built in the community by people being willing to step up and support others when they're tired, stressed or having to respond to another's need. Somebody quietly coming in to do the piles of washing up when they know that someone is becoming stressed about getting behind preparing a meal for 40 people is what builds our common life and it's not something you can really write into a job description.

The Post Office Horizon scandal where over 900 sub-postmasters were wrongfully convicted of stealing money from the organization because of computer errors is a stark illustration of an instance where belief in technology has been stronger than the organization's trust in its staff. It's a warning of the dangers of not knowing your staff and not listening to them and instead choosing to rely on the infallibility of a technical system. The subsequent cover-up was yet more scandalous and serves to further weaken people's trust in public bodies. When organizations don't trust their staff, it inevitably sets them against the organization, often leading to toxic relationships and poor performance. When profit and productivity is placed before the well-being of people, trust inevitably erodes. At Hilfield, where our economy is based on the quality of our life together, building trust with one another is a vital building block, and underpinning this is a foundational desire to trust in God.

Carmelite spirituality

Carmelite spirituality has at its heart this desire to grow in trust of God. The earliest Carmelites living around Mount Carmel, in what is now Israel, led lives of great simplicity, often dwelling in caves and learning to trust fully in God alone. The later sixteenth-century reforms of Teresa of Ávila and John of the Cross were an attempt to break down the elitism, divisions, complacency and wealth that was beginning to dilute the spiritual foundation of the order. Their reforms stressed the importance of simplicity in the Carmelite tradition, and their reformed houses were referred to as the 'Discalced Carmelites' as they went barefoot in their friaries and convents as a sign of their rejection of wealth, power and status. Teresa is famous for her prayer:

> Let nothing disturb you.
> Let nothing frighten you.
> All things pass.
> God never changes.
> Patience obtains all things.
> They who have God lack nothing.[1]

Her words reflect a faith that can be trusted and will sustain people in dark times. Both Teresa and John of the Cross faced strong opposition as reformers. John was imprisoned in a tiny cell in Toledo for nearly a year before his escape. For both of them, hardship and persecution led to a deeper reliance on God and their loyal Brothers and Sisters in the order. Writing about John of the Cross, Iain Matthews, a Carmelite Friar, speaks of a deep trust formed by adversity:

> Greater than the temple, greater than Jonah: God is greater than our feeling of God, greater than our concept of God. When our lights no longer offer support, when our sense of

> worth or place or progress is growing dim, when what should not be is – then a God who is greater than we are has room to impinge.[2]

Using the image of the dark night and what is not, John suggests we will find God through a persistent trust: 'the soul is not united to God in this life through understanding, or through enjoyments or through imagination, or through any other sense, but only faith, hope and charity can unite the soul with God in this life.'[3]

In the *Four Quartets*, T. S. Eliot famously quotes John:

> In order to arrive at what you do not know
> You must go by a way which is the way of ignorance.
> In order to possess what you do not possess
> You must go by the way of dispossession.
> In order to arrive at what you are not
> You must go through the way in which you are not.[4]

This way of negation is of course difficult as it's supressing the urges of our ego's need to achieve, but the way of sometimes blind trust is ultimately life-giving, as John says, 'When the soul enters the dark night all these loves are placed in reasonable order. This night strengthens and purifies the love that is of God and takes away and destroys the other.'[5]

Suffering loss and not having all the answers leads us to realize our need of others and, above all, God, which can be transformed to joy. Both Teresa and John are often described as full of gusto and delight in life. It's said that, as he lay dying, John asked his Brothers to stop reading from the Office for the Dying but instead read the love poetry of the Song of Songs.

Listening builds trust

John of the Cross was famous for his listening skills, and trust in community involves a commitment towards the others we live with and the willingness to keep listening. I know that when I've been really listened to, I'm left with a very pure kind of joy.

The best listeners are those who I can trust completely, who intuitively understand my vulnerabilities and who encourage me also to find and express my delight in life. Communities thrive when people feel valued and an essential part of building trust and belonging is regular opportunities to be listened to. When I became leader of the Pilsdon community, I offered each one of the community members an hour of supervision each month, or more regularly if it was required. Much of my supervision was focused around listening to people's joys and difficulties. I didn't do it out of a sense of altruism but out of pure self-interest. I knew that if I could further build the bonds of trust between myself and the community members, the daunting task of leading a complex community could be more readily shared. The community members had monthly meetings with guests to offer support, and the hope was that some of the listening I modelled would spread out into the community. Listening wasn't just limited to specific bounded times but of course happened in the daily round, perhaps sitting down on a journey to the doctors, chopping carrots in the kitchen or weeding the potato patch. Once a month, the community members would go for team supervision with an outside facilitator, which was a safe space in which to share difficulties in communication.

We also had a day together, every few years, exploring the Enneagram – a system based on ancient spiritual traditions which suggests nine different personality types, which you discover by examining your core motivations, desires and fears. It was good for me to discover I'm a number nine type – 'the Mediator' – but much more useful to know the predominant type of my fellow community members, as it helped me understand why I found certain people difficult and, more importantly, why they found me challenging to live with. Knowing someone was a one – 'the Perfectionist' – encouraged me to tidy up assiduously in areas I knew they would be working. Seeing a number seven – 'the Enthusiast' – preparing a meal with great energy filled me with joy at seeing their intense sense of fulfilment. It was a tool that helped us examine and delight in our differences, often provoking a lot of fun – 'Yes you're being a typical "nine", late again?' It helped us grow in understanding and compassion for one another.

Shared challenges and embracing risk can build trust

At Pilsdon, we occasionally had some difficult and dangerous situations to sort out with highly manipulative people, so it was essential that the community members knew and trusted each other. One evening a guest started a fire in three different parts of the manor house, which we couldn't put out. They then took an overdose, which meant all three emergency services arrived in one night. The trust we had for each other helped us get through a long and difficult night, but it also deepened through our shared experience of crisis. The wider community too seemed strengthened by coping with the threat to it.

My association with Christian Climate Action, Insulate Britain and Just Stop Oil has taught me about the need for trust when taking risky and sometimes unpopular actions. Embedded in the non-violent methodologies of all these organizations has been the chance to listen to one another. Every Zoom meeting begins with a 'check in', which allows people to have a couple of minutes to say how they are. The night before an action there is a time where people will again voice fears and excitement and commit to trusting one another in putting their bodies on the line. The actions themselves can feel fraught with danger, blocking hostile motorists, disrupting events, breaking the law and not knowing what the legal and financial penalties will be. After actions, if people aren't in custody there's an opportunity to debrief. People will also run training sessions on some of the deeper philosophy of non-violence, or sessions on meditation and yoga, and people also offer listening circles where fear, anger, grief and other difficult emotions can be heard and safely held.

Paul Lederach says,

> I have increasingly come to believe that listening is not about technique or paraphrasing but about aesthetics. Listening, if understood from this direction, is akin to a haiku attitude and the haiku moment. Listening is the discipline and art of capturing the complexity of history in the simplicity of deep intuition. It is attending to a sharp sense of what things mean.[6]

The more I listen to people in spiritual accompaniment, the more I learn to trust my instinct, sometimes to sit with people in silence and let them speak out of it, sometimes to risk a question that has popped into my head and seems a little different. It feels much more like an art than a science, a receiving more than a giving out. When preparing to lead a workshop I've learned to risk leaving space for people, to trust them to come up with ideas and trust in the collective wisdom of the group rather than teach didactically. This way the group can go in the direction it needs to go, not the way I want to lead it into.

Building trust through encounter

In 2024, I'm revisiting the West Bank with 82-year-old Revd Sue Parfitt, who has asked me to go and carry her bags. On our first morning we are looking for Wi'am, a centre for peace and reconciliation that I remembered was close to the eight-metre-high grey concrete wall that surrounds much of Bethlehem. We know we've arrived when we see a sign that reads: 'You are welcome to visit Wi'am Centre – make coffee/tea, not walls'.

We are invited in by the inspirational Zoughbi Zoughbi, a large, gentle and avuncular man. He offers us strong Palestinian coffee flavoured with cardamom, but our conversation is strangely subdued. Sue and I prepare to leave, but not before I ask Zoughbi how he copes with his anger at the situation in Bethlehem, which has effectively been locked down by the Israeli military, and the far greater suffering of the people of Gaza. 'Good question,' he replies. He reflects for a moment then says, 'I don't know the answer' and suddenly he becomes animated, 'Call all the staff and volunteers, let's have a workshop.'

His team gathers around and he facilitates the group. He begins by saying how destructive anger can be, how it leads to increased blood pressure and one man tells how a member of his family had a heart attack as he was so distressed by watching news from Gaza. He says anger can create an unhealthy atmosphere and lead to violence and how if it is internalized it can lead to depression. He then goes on to say how anger can be positive if it is harnessed and how it can be transformed for good. Then he returns to my question and asks us in turn to share how we cope with anger. One woman says she smashes things, another person how he goes for long walks, somebody else plays loud music, someone soothing classical tunes, another person cries, another expresses it in a supportive group, another reads the Koran, another quotes from Ephesians 4 – 'Be angry but do not sin' (Eph. 4.26). The answer I like best comes from a man who says, 'I go and plant a tree as a positive action.' Someone tells the story of building the children's playground in the centre's small garden as a peaceful act of resistance against the violence that surrounds everybody's life. It's a dynamic hour and at the end of it Zoughbi breaks into a huge smile and says thank you for the question and we leave energized by what's been a difficult, but transformative meeting. Later on, I read about 'Sulha', an ancient Arabic way of mediation adapted by Zoughbi for his daily peacemaking work. The practice is to seek a third-party mediator when there is conflict between two people. The mediator will spend time listening to each person and also crucially to their extended families. When both parties are ready to listen to each other, then a meeting is arranged and people meet and if peace is established it will be sealed by both families sitting down to drink coffee together. The aim of Sulha is to replace mutual derision with feelings of mutual solidarity, and build respect and good relationships. It works if people are prepared to step out of their resentments and certainties about the 'other'.

In *The Poisonwood Bible*, Barbara Kingsolver contrasts the certainty and biblical fundamentalism of Nathan with another long-term missionary, Brother Fowles, who suggests that we

> trust in Creation which is made fresh daily and doesn't suffer in translation. This god does not work in especially mysterious ways. The sun here rises and sets at 6 exactly. A caterpillar becomes a butterfly. A bird raises its brood in the forest and a green leaf tree will grow from a Greenleaf seed.[7]

Trusting in nature

Living close to the land helps build this trust in creation, but also in one another; there is something about the order, rhythms and interconnected systems in nature that, as well as giving us places of green sanctuary and calm, model ways of interconnectivity that human society so desperately needs to build. Might daring to trust in the natural rhythms of decay and repair we see in nature give us a clue how to slowly build up society, by using a model not of control and forced growth, but a slower more dynamic and organic model? Here rewilding has a lot to teach us about trusting natural organic systems to find healthy ways of regenerating life. In the 1970s, the catchphrase 'Plant a tree in '73' was an encouragement for people and public bodies to go out and plant trees to improve the look of their localities and also suck in carbon dioxide. It's estimated that only one fifth of those trees survived to become mature specimens. In contrast, when you fence off a bit of land to keep cattle, sheep and deer out, trees will grow far more efficiently, by the method of simply doing nothing. First will come brambles and other primary thorny colonizers; trees will seed in the most fertile patches protected by this scrub and eventually form new woodland, fast-growing trees coming first then the more long-lasting durable specimens like oaks will come more slowly.

At Knepp Castle Estate, a failing mixed 3,000-acre farm, which had high inputs of fertilizers and pesticides and heavy farm machinery and many human hours of toil, was fenced off and left to revert to its natural state. Large herbivores, Longhorn cows, Tamworth pigs and Dartmoor ponies were introduced to help break open the ground and move seeds around on their hairy bodies. In just five years the landscape was transformed. Turtle doves can once more be heard, and the purple emperor butterfly has taken up residence. The farm had gone from a business producing large amounts of carbon dioxide to a valuable carbon sink and through ecotourism and renting out former buildings for farm machinery is now making a healthy profit. Trusting natural systems to regenerate themselves is one way forward in allowing us to live more sustainably. Often less is more.

Wendell Berry, in his Jefferson Lecture of 2011 'It All Turns on Affection', contrasts 'boomers' and 'stickers'. 'Boomers' are those who pillage and run and are motivated by greed and expansion, whereas 'stickers' are motivated by affection for a place and its life. I would suggest that 'boomers' are contractual people whereas 'stickers' are more covenantal types, more interested in trust and relationships than creating wealth. The creation of common wealth, including non-human life rather than monetary value, will build trust as opposed to competition and fragmentation. Berry writes, 'as imagination enables sympathy, sympathy enables affection. And it is in affection that we find the possibility of a neighbourly, kind and conserving economy.'[8] A hundred years ago, Wendell Berry's grandfather stuck with his principles, didn't sell his farm, trusted in the land and Berry today continues to farm regeneratively.

Uncomplicated trust

At Pilsdon, if someone was going through a difficult time we would sometimes take them to our neighbour Bill's land to collect wood. Bill was in his 70s and bent over from years of toil. He had sold his dairy cattle but continued looking after his land with a few beef cattle simply for the love of it. Dressed in his black beret and brown cotton work coat tied with bailer twine and hunched over his 1950s Massey Ferguson tractor, he seemed forever fixed in the landscape. His land was a bit wild in contrast to the heavily industrialized fields surrounding it and I went over to help him manage his hedges, but it was always Bill helping me and whoever I took with me. I trusted him to be gentle and kind with whoever I took, but more so I trusted the fields and hedgerow to bring comfort to whoever I took for the day. For many who came to Pilsdon with their minds fractured by the pressures of urban life, contact with the soil and animals as much as the healthy patterns we lived by helped them towards recovery. Those who'd experienced various traumas, particularly sexual abuse, found it difficult to trust anyone, but the uncomplicated constancy of the cows, the pigs or the donkeys helped them restore some sense that parts of the world were good. The elderly and rather battered donkeys Peter and Paul who'd retired from Weymouth beach 30 years ago seemed particularly good at lifting people out of despair and isolation.

Some General Practitioners now do social prescribing, rather than writing a script for drugs. They might suggest time at a gardening project, a wildlife charity or rambling club. For some, what's known as 'wild swimming' in cold lakes, rivers and seas is an effective way of fighting off depression by encouraging the body to produce endorphins. As Brother Fowles said, 'Trust in creation.'

Daring to not know

Trusting in what's seen and surrounds us engenders our sense of belonging to a place and the natural world, but being able to trust in the hidden, and trusting to be empty, is more challenging. I think what sustains me most in community is sometimes daring to be empty, to give up and to risk being nothing. Blind trust. Suffering loss and not being in control can lead us to growth through learning to know our need for the trust and support of others. Learning we can't do it all on our own is one of the great gifts of living in community.

At Pilsdon, a newly arrived community member was in floods of tears after midday prayers. I was concerned, so I sat with her quietly in the church waiting for her to speak. 'I just can't do this, it's impossible, there's too much pain being carried here, it's too much!' she told me through more tears. 'Ahh,' I gently replied, 'you've learnt the first and most important lesson of Pilsdon. It is too much, we can't do it on our own. That's why we need each other and most of all to trust in God. It shouldn't work here, you're right but somehow it does.' She smiled at me, nodding, and we went into lunch. She stayed, and was a valued member of the community for a number of years. What I began to learn at Pilsdon was to accept the limits of my own agency, to not worry too much about what could go wrong, and when situations became stressful to try and deal with things with an outward equanimity. To keep trusting in the people around me, particularly the other community members and know that others had been here before me and Pilsdon had survived. The longer I was there and the more tense situations we came through the easier it was to believe this. The thing that helped most was the time spent doing nothing in the chapel. It was the pattern of becoming still and the emptying of contemplative prayer that resourced both me and the community.

John of the Cross writes, 'Through this contemplation, God teaches the soul secretly and instructs it in the perfection of love without its doing anything or understanding how this happens.'[9]

Daring to be empty, to not know, to still the mind in its endless rushing around for solutions and instead trust in the waiting can help us discern the way to move forward purposefully both as individuals and communities. Evagrius, writing in the fourth century, talks about prayer being 'the laying aside of thoughts'.[10]

The process of emptying ourselves of thoughts enables us to escape the domination of our false self and the power of ego and the individualism that can be so destructive of community. Stopping and doing nothing helps us to regain a sense of right purpose. I've learnt, when struggling and swearing at a task at Hilfield, that it's much better to give up and go and pray when I hear the chapel bell tolling, rather than try and push on. So often when I return to the job I do so with fresh energy and a solution pops into my mind. So too we're learning as a community when facing a difficult and complex decision, that often the wisest thing is to step back from it, agreeing to return to it in a few days' time and when we do we have a deeper and better discussion and more consensual decision.

Not knowing just trusting

In the Christian tradition the day that expresses 'not knowing' as sacred space is Holy Saturday, which lies between Good Friday and Easter. Most churches fail to mark it, instead filling the day with preparations for Easter – busily polishing candlesticks and cramming the smell of flowers into the churches rather than leaving empty space. The activity feels like the typical human response: to try and fill the void of death, baking cakes for the bereaved and trying to cheer up the grieving rather than just sitting quietly with their and our own pain. At Pilsdon a lot of people had come to us as a result of trauma – what you might describe as their Good Friday – and were waiting for some kind of renewal, their Easter, which left them in a liminal place, betwixt and between, a place of not knowing or their Holy Saturday. So on the Saturday before Easter we sought to honour this by keeping the church empty for the morning and then in the late afternoon silently but corporately constructing a stone tomb with an old millstone as its entrance. Slowly, and mindfully, grass and primroses would be dug up and placed around the place of death. There was a waiting.

Thomas Keating captures well the importance of such an emptying:

> We are made for happiness and there is nothing wrong with reaching out for it. Unfortunately most of us are so deprived of happiness that as soon as it does come along we reach out for it with all our strength and try to hang on to it for dear life. That is the mistake. The best way to receive it is to give it away. If you give everything back to God, you will always be empty and when you are empty there is more room for God.[11]

Emptiness can help us discern our way forward as communities, busyness in contrast often helps us lose our way. For the Carmelites, it's faith before works and action arising out of contemplation. Stephen Wright, a contemplative working on the spiritual underpinnings of deep adaptation, writes,

> This is the contemplative way, plumbing the depths of the inner life in order to discover the resources to act with fierce equanimity in the outer. That enables us to do differently, be differently. Unlike commercialism and materialism compassionate service is not measured by volume. There is no big or small. One loving act equals the whole. Even the tiniest kiss of love on the cheek of suffering is worth it.[12]

In the middle of the small oak-panelled house chapel at Pilsdon sits the hub of an old cart wheel. In its centre a candle is lit each night for Compline and it represents that still point in a revolving world that if we can find it brings peace and unity. A unity John of the Cross captures:

> The tranquil night
> At the time of the rising dawn,
> Silent music,
> Sounding solitude,
> The supper that refreshes, and deepens love.[13]

Out of silence can come the desire to be more fully present and feast with others. Paradoxically silence builds community and allows us to reach out to others, particularly those in need.

Questions

1. Who in the Bible exemplifies trust and why?
2. Who do I trust the most and what gives me confidence in them?
3. How many of my relationships with people and groups are covenantal and how many are contractual?
4. What erodes trust in society?
5. How might I build and increase trust with friends, neighbours and those I disagree with?

Practical suggestions

1. Read up on Carmelite spirituality.
2. Embrace a more contemplative way of praying, such as contemplativeoutreach.org.uk.

3 Make an intention to share a bit more from your own vulnerability with those you trust.

4 Be part of a group that allows you to be listened to and lets you listen to others.

5 Trust in the restorative power of nature.

Notes

1 Teresa of Ávila writing in the margin of her breviary. See Carmelite Spirit, n.d., 'Let Nothing Disturb You?', *Carmelite Spirit*, https://carmelite.com/let-nothing-disturb-you/, accessed 21.01.2026.

2 Iain Matthews, 2009, *The Impact of God*, London: Hodder and Stoughton, p. 85.

3 John of the Cross, 1987, *Selected Writings*, Kieren Kavanagh (ed.), New York: Paulist Press, p. 93.

4 T. S. Eliot, 1951, *Four Quartets*, London: Faber and Faber, p. 20.

5 John of the Cross, *Selected Writings*, p. 172.

6 Paul Lederach, 2007, *The Moral Imagination*, Oxford: Oxford University Press, p. 76.

7 Barbara Kingsolver, 2000, *The Poisonwood Bible*, London: Faber and Faber, p. 279.

8 Wendell Berry, 2012, *'It All turns on Affection': The Jefferson Lecture and other Essays*, Berekley, CA: Counterpoint Press, p. 8.

9 John of the Cross, *Selected Writings*, p. 201.

10 Evagrius 70. 1973, in E. Kadloubovsky and G. E. H. Palmer (eds and trans.), *The Philokalia*, 5th edn, London: Faber and Faber, p. 83.

11 Thomas Keating, 2003, *Open Mind, Open Heart*, New York: Continuum, p. 88.

12 Stephen Wright, 2023, *Fugue: Climate, Collapse and Contemplation*, Cumbria: Sacred Space, p. 125.

13 John of the Cross, *Selected Writings*, p. 223.

6

Need

It's 4.30am on a Saturday and I'm filling a five-gallon thermos flask with a large tap on it with 40 tea bags, boiling water, two pints of milk and finally half a bag of sugar. We load it through the sliding doors of a faded blue VW transporter van, alongside two large trays stacked with either jam or cheese sandwiches, made with bread donated by a Jewish bakery, buttered the previous night as it closed for Shabbat. It's for the Simon Community 'Tea Run' and we're heading for three destinations in central London where we know we'll be expected. I rev up the engine, clean the frost off the windscreen and we drive through quiet streets. It's 1981 and as I turn on the radio, we hear Neil Young's falsetto singing 'There was a band playing in my head and I felt like getting high' and we know there'll be plenty we meet under the influence of drink or drugs as we try and deliver a little comfort to some of London's homeless.

We arrive at Dean Street, where we stop outside the Labour Exchange. Homeless men are queuing up, looking for casual work and glad of hot tea and an early breakfast. Then on to the back of the Strand Palace Hotel where rough sleepers have been keeping warm by sleeping on the horizontal iron railings that vent warm air out of the building. For them it's a chance for food and company before the police and road-sweeping vehicles move them on. Our last stop is Lincoln's Inn Fields, a park outside one of the Inns of Court, which wealthy lawyers will confidently stride through later in the day. I park and, as others are handing out tea and food to those emerging in the half light, I speak to 'Jerusalem', an elderly man with a large black hat, thick black wool winter coat and a long white beard and gleaming eyes like 'The Ancient of Days'. He tells me what the weather will be for the week (he's invariably right), then, looking at the van, he reminds me, as he always does: 'The VW engine – a 39-piece engine, a miracle of modern engineering.' Once everyone's had hot sweet tea and a sandwich or bagel, it's my task today to hand out the smokes. People quietly form a circle, someone hands out cigarette papers and into the paper and onto opened hands I deposit a generous pinch of tobacco. It makes me think of Communion, those hands reaching out in need of sustenance.

Just as we're about to go, someone shouts urgently, 'Ginger's in the bushes. I think he's a goner.' We go over and find a man with frost in his flaming hair and stiff with the cold. He's still breathing – just. He tells us he feels warm and we recognize this as hypothermia setting in. It's the days before you called an ambulance for everything, so four of us pick him up as he's a dead weight, wrap him in blankets and wedge him into the front seat, turn on the heaters and force him to drink tea. We get him back to the Night Shelter, turn up the central heating and he is soon restored, breakfasting with the rest of the Simon Community crew.

Simon Community was founded in 1963 by Anton Wallich Clifford, a probation officer at Bow Street Magistrates Court, who kept seeing the same faces of homeless men coming before the courts charged with minor offences. He resolved to do something and set up a house of hospitality seeking to respond to the needs of homeless people by providing a safe place for people to be. The Simon Community took people who couldn't – or wouldn't – fit into more institutional forms of care, be it because of their poor mental health, anti-social behaviour, out-of-control drinking, or outspokenness. Each house had three simple rules: no drink, no drugs, no violence on the premises. You would still be accepted if you were drunk but had to leave your bottle at the door or surrender it to the house safe. The year I was there, there was surprisingly little violence considering how much some people had drunk before they arrived at the night shelter, but when it did occur, we managed it through banding together as a household and quickly removing the person. More testing was welcoming people with complex mental health needs, but again the high levels of acceptance in the houses and the daily routines seemed to allow people to feel relatively safe. The volunteer workers would sleep on the floor of the houses while the homeless would sleep in the beds. As a 19-year-old volunteer, I learnt a huge amount about addiction, self-harm, psychotic illness, anxiety and depression, but most of all how human kindness and common solidarity are what people on the margins, and indeed all of us, most need.

Responding to need is part of being human

Anton used to say that when someone is stuck in a hole in the ground, most services would throw a rope down and tell them to climb out, but at Simon we climb down into the hole with them and clamber out together. He said, 'We must see Christ in every shattered body' and must be prepared like Simon of Cyrene to walk alongside them and help carry their cross for a while, hence the name. When I reflect on it now, lifting Ginger out of the bushes at Lincoln's Inn Fields feels like a kind of tableau of Christ being taken down from the cross.

Simon was all about responding to need, not in a systematic or controlling way but in a way that was intensely human and compassionate. The community's response to people in crisis was more about being with them than providing services for them. More about solidarity than rehabilitation. We were about a radical hospitality that provided safe places where people felt loved and respected as our guests, not service users. For several years after I left the community, when travelling across London I would still bump into homeless people I knew from Simon, sometimes begging or drinking at a train station and we'd stop and exchange greetings, a bit of community for me in the anonymous city. Simon taught me to respond to the needs of others in a compassionate, non-judgemental way and showed me a way of being a Christian that put the suffering of the marginalized right at its heart.

The inspiration of the Catholic Worker Movement

Simon Community was inspired by the Catholic Worker Movement started by Dorothy Day and Peter Maurin in New York in 1933, which sought through 'works of mercy' – feeding the hungry, sheltering the homeless, visiting prisoners and establishing Houses of Hospitality – to live out what Peter Maurin called the 'Manifesto of the Gospels'. Today there are over 150 Catholic Worker Houses around the world where people live in community supporting destitute people. It was said of Dorothy Day that 'she comforted the afflicted and afflicted the comfortable' because not only did Catholic Worker communities feed the poor but also asked why they were poor and campaigned strongly for peace and justice. Dorothy was arrested a number of times for non-violent direct action. Catholic Worker spirituality stresses the importance of meeting Christ in the needs of the hungry and marginalized:

> We must practice the presence of God. He is in the midst of us and he is with us in our kitchens, at our tables, on our breadlines, with our visitors. When we pray for our material needs, it brings us close to his humanity. He too needed food and shelter. He warmed his hands at a fire and lay down in a boat to sleep.[1]

This echoes St Benedict's earlier words: 'The greatest care should be taken to welcome the poor and pilgrims, because it is in them above all others that Christ is welcomed. As for the rich they have a way of exacting respect.'[2]

For both Benedict and Dorothy, the works of mercy came from a place of picturing Christ among the weakest and most vulnerable, which in turn grew out of a lifetime of devotional prayer. Dorothy would attend mass daily, pray the rosary and spend up to two hours a day meditating on the Scriptures in silence. Hers was a life of costly care for the poor, marching for peace and justice and going to prison, but underpinning her activism was a daily practice of contemplation, which resourced her and her work:

> You must know when to find your own quiet moment of solitude. But you must know when to open the door to go to be with others, and you must know how to open the door. There is no point opening the door with bitterness and resentment in your heart.[3]

Nearly 100 years since their foundation, Catholic Worker communities continue to be formed, always as a response to great need, often today working with destitute asylum seekers and refugees. They owe their continued existence to the fact that responding to need can galvanize a community and builds up trust and a sense of interdependence between community members, inspired by common values that are being acted out.

Responding to need can strengthen community bonds

The challenges and stresses of responding to people in great need can only be sustained by learning to depend on one another. Working with people who are homeless, traumatized or vulnerable reminds us of our own needs and deepens a sense of human solidarity.

While visiting Bethlehem and Hebron with Sue Parfitt we noticed that the people we met were under great psychological and economic stress, and perhaps because of this they lived with huge regard for one another and intense solidarity. I was reminded so much of my Romany Gypsy friends who have similar bonds of community, also born out of the need to survive in a hostile environment. In Bethlehem, we would get into a taxi to go somewhere, and it would become obvious that the driver didn't know where we were going, but in a way he did, because he'd immediately get on the phone and ring one of his extended family or friends who would tell him the way. It felt very like asking for help from one of my Traveller friends, who if they couldn't assist themselves, would immediately be on the phone to a cousin or friend who would come up with a solution. Reflecting on this, I drew out other similarities, the love of the land and outdoors, a history of marginalization and being moved on from the land, forced settlement, disproportional numbers of their community being in prison, high degrees of stress and poor mental health. Strongest though was the sense of resilience, the importance of the extended families and networks of support to survive a world stacked against them. The Palestinians call this resilience 'Sumud'; Travellers say, 'They've been trying to get rid of us for years but we'll keep our culture alive in spite of all the prejudice and attempts to destroy our way of life.'

Romany Gypsy customs around death show that the community knows how to come together to support others in times of crisis. When someone from the community dies, members of the extended family will immediately visit and in the days leading up to the funeral the bereaved family will never be left alone, there will always be visitors in the house. The night before the funeral, 'Sitting Up' happens. The body of the deceased will be brought back and left in an open casket, often in a caravan, back room or large tent in the back garden. Often hundreds of people will visit to pay their respects, comfort the family and view the body. Traditionally, the women will sit indoors drinking tea and offering food and the men will stand outside around a fire which will burn all night. The next day people will gather at the house to form a procession to follow the coffin and truck-loads of flowers to the church. Often horses are used to pull the hearse and flatbeds full of elaborate floral displays. At the graveside there's a great scrum of people often singing favourite songs of the deceased, and powerful outpourings of grief. Once the grave is filled in, people will gather at a hall or pub. Hundreds of people will turn out and it's a huge public spectacle of community solidarity. This stands in contrast to 'direct cremation', which is growing in popularity among the settled community. Here the body of the deceased travels alone to the crematorium, and later a small gathering of friends and immediate family might come together in a front room for a rather muted gathering.

The importance of hospitality

Learning how to respond well to need fosters interdependence, and extending hospitality to those in need builds a common sense of kinship. At Hilfield Friary, during the 2020 lockdown brought on by the spread of Covid-19, we were insulated from the most isolating and limiting effects of government restrictions by the fact we lived in a bubble of 27 people and had a 'garden' of 45 acres. We still maintained the prayers in the chapel, we fed the animals, tended the garden, repaired buildings and cooked for each other. For some in the community it was like an extended holiday as our major work is welcoming guests, and yet the community felt strangely flat. We began to realize that we needed our guests to bring in energy from outside and give us a sense of purpose. Without people to host we were just a bunch of people living together in a very privileged and sheltered existence. If the state of lockdown had continued, having so little contact with the outside world would have led to the disintegration of the Hilfield Community, as without a need to respond to we would have lost our outward-looking Franciscan focus. If a community solely exists for the benefit of its members and defends its borders too much, it's likely to become stale and people are likely to become more and more concerned with fulfilling their own needs at the expense of the common good.

At Pilsdon it was wonderful to see a recently arrived guest welcoming another new arrival, giving them a tour, showing them how everything worked and giving them tips about community life. There was no front door or reception; you entered through the farmyard and you'd have to ask someone the way to get in, and you'd be ushered into the aga room where someone would make you tea, welcoming you into the hearth. We never trained anyone how to receive new guests, but so strong was the culture of welcome that everyone picked it up. So many people at Pilsdon had arrived in crisis or great need that they instinctively knew how to gently and sensitively draw people into our common life. The warmest welcome was reserved for the wayfarers who'd usually walked the seven miles from Bridport. Sometimes bedraggled and often smelling of stale alcohol, they'd be welcomed in for tea, someone would supply a roll-up and show them to the laundry where they could pick up clean sheets and wash clothes, after being fitted out with a fresh set from the 'boutique', a shed with donated clothing. At supper, the wayfarers ate at the table with everyone else, would always be first to be offered a second helping and were invited to wash up to show they were fully part of the community, for the night or the weekend they were with us. Many were regular visitors and received as old friends, others coming for the first time would be gently folded into the community. Sometimes their needs were complex, people's behaviour could be unsettling and conversations could be bizarre, but as long as they observed the community's boundaries they'd be welcome. The best hosts to the wayfarers were those who'd been on the road themselves. George Culshaw, a former Royal Marine and retired 'roadman' with an open and generous heart, was an enthusiastic sweeper of the courtyard. Because of this he would often be the first to greet the wayfarers, always sharing tobacco, with old friends or newcomers. His was a kind of Bedouin hospitality intuitively knowing the needs of the traveller.

Responding to need builds community and brings us close to the heart of the divine. R. S. Thomas articulates this so well in his poem 'The Kingdom', where he suggests that 'you present yourself with your need only' in order to enter the freedom of God's kingdom.[4]

Meeting real needs

What people found at Pilsdon was an antidote to many of the cravings of our consumer-driven culture, where artificial needs are generated by an advertising industry that creates what Bruce Wilshire calls 'Wild Hunger'. Wiltshire argues that we have come so far from our hunter-gatherer roots that the former natural highs produced by surviving from the land have been replaced by things that no longer satisfy. These artificial highs only satisfy briefly, leading to the desire for a further hit of shopping, drugs, alcohol or pornography and thus we enter into cycles of addiction. The way out for him is recognizing this and expanding our connection to the natural world. Pilsdon offered a safe place to reject these 'hungry ghosts' and their destructive power, by offering security and solid encounter with nature through work with animals, work on the land and work in the garden. The only people who didn't fit into the embrace of Pilsdon were those who weren't willing to admit their vulnerability and need of others. Those who were too proud or defensive to admit they needed help never seemed to do too well and Pilsdon's deep culture of acceptance could never really touch them as they weren't able to admit their fallibilities. Pilsdon's founder Percy Smith wrote in one of his Letters to Community, 'Occasionally people arrive who have not told the truth about themselves, and Pilsdon seems a very hard, unrelenting and even unloving place.'[5]

Knowing our own needs

As well as offering the gift of responding to others, community teaches us the perhaps harder lesson of recognizing our own needs. Like George, we welcome people warmly when we remember our own past needs for food, for shelter, for company. To do this well and over a sustained time it's important we have an awareness of our own needs and we don't seek to fulfil them through helping or seeking to rescue others. Not understanding this can lead us to becoming annoyingly helpful or result in fatigue and burnout. Alongside our positive inclinations can also be more negative projections as people we live with trigger our own unresolved conflict, what R. S. Thomas would describe as our 'furious interiors'.

During lockdown I was rather alarmed to discover I began to experience feelings of intense dislike and hostility towards three members of the community. I felt disturbed by the anger and disgust I felt towards people with whom I was supposed to be living in community. I knew that lockdown had reduced us to a more settled and less transient community so there was a much more intense focus on each other. The distraction of working outside the community was also no longer there for me. I began to understand that our guests were sometimes used by the community and me to project blame onto. As they moved on from us, they, like nomadic people, were convenient scapegoats on which we could dump our unresolved difficulties with ourselves and each other. I forced myself to be civil to the three I was struggling with, and knew from my experience of living at Pilsdon, where I'd had to learn to process difficult feelings provoked by others, that I could work through things. The feelings were so powerful that I knew they were a projection of my own unresolved conflicts and I was aware I had to do the shadow work, to heal the rage in me.

Jung describes our shadow as pure gold and if we can become conscious of the difficult feelings it reveals we can grow into more integrated people. The Dalai Lama has said your enemy is your greatest teacher, for if we take the time to work through our difficulties with others and see what they are triggering in us, we can grow in compassion for them and also those parts of ourselves we don't like. The Buddhist practice of loving-kindness was a particularly helpful tool in promoting this reconciliation with others and my own unprocessed feelings. It involves working through a meditation, imagining cultivating kindness first to yourself, then a friend, then a relative stranger, then someone you find difficult and finally to all beings. It's a powerful yet gentle way of breaking down barriers between people and realizing our fundamental unity as human beings.

One of the three people I found most difficult was somebody who was demanding that the community operated under the strictest quarantine rules, much more than the government advice for Covid-19. I'd often resented what I saw as his lack of commitment to the community and his unwillingness to go beyond the clearly defined area of work and role he'd assigned for himself in the community. When I heard myself quite out of character saying in a meeting he wasn't at that 'I felt like punching his effing face in', I immediately recognized this as something from my shadow, and realized I had work to do. The next meeting I apologized and told everyone how ashamed I was of using such violent language – me, a peace activist committed to nonviolence! Over the next few days, I was able to realize that my reaction came out of some very old unresolved feelings of being constrained and feeling I had to obey certain unwritten rules as a child. I was also able to see some of the fear he felt as one of the less fit members of the community about becoming ill, and have compassion for this. Looking at his carefully set up boundaries around work and leisure was also a lesson to me, as someone who tends to overwork in a somewhat undisciplined way. For this I was enormously grateful, and I was able to express real warmth to him. Everyone, even the most unlikely people, can mentor us if we are prepared to let them.

Rumi, in his poem 'The Guest House', captures the gift of welcoming in our difficult feelings and urges us to

> Meet them at the door laughing
> And invite them in.[6]

If we're prepared to notice, there's often a gift of self-understanding offered to us by those we find most difficult.

We need support from others

Sometimes we can't work through our difficulties on our own and there's a need to share our vulnerability and not be afraid to ask for support. Life in community, living in voluntary poverty and living with people on the edge of society taught Dorothy Day to seek help from others and share her vulnerability. As she writes, 'To speak truth, to have the courage to say that you need the help of others to get you through, to hold you, to face up to life with, this is the treasure we can find here.'[7] Knowing our own frailties and vulnerabilities and from this place reaching out to others from a place of recognizing some of our needs in theirs can form a precious and genuine human solidarity. It's an invitation to live in a different economy that breaks down hierarchy and a sense of separateness so embedded in our highly defended culture.

Writing in *The Guardian*, Emma Beddington describes the Norwegian concept of *dugnadsånd*, roughly translated as 'community spirit', as something we might do well to adopt in increasingly lonely Britain. Key to *dugnadsånd* is the recognition of our own limitations and the need for support of others. Once we do this and ask for the help of others, a new kind of community spirit is born:

> It is intimate, also vulnerable, to accept and express when we need help; to want to offer it but not know how or to feel inept when we do; to accept we need another. *Dugnadsånd* – practical solidarity, really – seems like a way of practising that, of training our collective thinking, collective action, but also training our collective vulnerability muscles.[8]

Emma writes about something people in indigenous communities have always known, that to survive we need the support of others.

Breaking down of mutual support

Sadly, in many parts of Britain old networks of support are breaking down and populist politicians and far-right groups are encouraging impoverished and marginalized communities to blame particular groups for their predicament. People's lack of good jobs, affordable housing, good schools and health provision isn't because of uncontrolled immigration and people fleeing violence and persecution in small boats, but rather an economic system and decades of government policy that create wealth for the few and promote inequality. Groups like the English Defence League and Reform recruit members by creating convenient scapegoats – persuading people that others are taking what should be theirs by right, particularly targeting those whose needs aren't being met.

In August 2024, a few days after the murder of three young girls in Southport by Axel Rudakubana, who was wrongly identified as a Muslim asylum seeker, riots broke out throughout the country. I went to a counter-demonstration in Weymouth organized by 'Dorset Stand Up to Racism'. We were separated from a far-right group by the police whose line gradually got thinner as the tide receded from the beach. There were the inevitable tub-thumping speeches by Trade Unionists and leftist activists and then the chanting began: 'Whose streets? Our streets!' 'Off our streets, you Nazi scum!'

After half an hour of this, I began to feel quite uncomfortable with the anger and what felt like the latent violence of the counter-protest. I turned to Giovanna, a lifelong non-violent activist and campaigner for justice, who said, 'I'm going if they don't shut up, let's see if we can get everyone to sit down and be silent for a bit.' We tried to negotiate this, but people were enjoying the moral condemnation too much. Rather than jeering at largely ordinary disenfranchised people, wouldn't it be better to go and talk to them, we thought? But the police line was stopping us. Most people supporting far-right narratives aren't heartless thugs, but people who haven't been listened to, and people whose needs haven't been met. Reading some of the transcripts of those coming before the courts following the August 2024 riots, it becomes clear that many of those involved did not do so from an ideological standpoint, but simply got caught up in the anger and drama of the event.

Healthy communities are those that listen to the needs of each person within the community and reach out to those in need outside of its bounds, and in this way model inclusion and interdependence. So often in my experience it's the stranger or person from a different culture who brings the blessing of new insight or reminds me that community is built around hospitality and listening to the needs of others.

The needs of the natural world

Slowly I'm learning to listen to the needs of the natural world too. To look at the sheep and recognize if one is acting differently and then check it for fly strike, worms or foot problems. With the cows, to notice if their udders are bagging up, indicating a calf will come soon. Watching the comb on the chicken's head, knowing if it starts to droop or the bright red begins to fade that something may be amiss. To notice plants and begin to intuit as much as empirically observe that they are stressed and perhaps need water or feeding with some nutrients. Watching trees become stressed by hotter and hotter summers, blown over by high summer winds or slowly perishing from imported ash dieback, all point to the threat of the climate crisis and the degradation of nature.

We won't be able to prevent these reverses if we don't notice and learn to love the created order. As Thomas Berry says, we need to learn to see the natural world as a communion of subjects rather than a collection of objects. To rejoice in the added biodiversity that comes when we plant a hedge or leave a bit of land to recover naturally and to notice too my growing friendship with the landscape and particularly the mature trees as I recognize their healing effect on me. Thomas Merton, a Cistercian monk, hermit and a friend of Dorothy Day, writes from a place of recognizing the divine in nature and its healing intimacy:

> The silence of the forest is my bride and the sweet dark warmth of the whole world is my love and out of the heart of that dark warmth comes the secret that is only heard in silence, but it is the root of all the secrets that are whispered by all their lovers in their beds all over the world.[9]

I'm learning that my needs as they are met and nourished by a whole network of people and communities are also met by the wider more-than-human landscape/community of which I'm part. I'm slowly coming to grasp the importance of simple manual work in helping me gain a sense of belonging to the wider world and the people I live with.

Questions

1 What are some of the classic biblical texts about responding to those in need?

2 How does encounter with people in need affect and challenge you?

3 Have you ever had the experience of receiving the support of others when facing particularly daunting challenges?

4 How do you cope with difficult people?

5 How do you process difficult feelings?

Practical suggestions

1 Learn about the Catholic Worker Movement: catholicworker.org.

2 Think about supporting work with refugees: sanctuaryfoundation.org.uk.

3 Think about supporting work with Gypsies, Roma and Travellers: sanctuaryplaces.co.uk.

4 Try out the practice of loving-kindness: thebuddhistcentre.com.

5 Read about reconnecting with the divine in nature: soulrewilding.co.uk.

Notes

1 Dorothy Day, 2005, *Selected Writings*, London: Darton, Longman and Todd, p. 92.

2 Timothy Fry (trans.), 1982, *The Rule of St Benedict*, Collegeville, MN: Liturgical Press, p. 74.

3 Jeffrey Odell Korgen, 2024, *Radical Devotion*, Mahwah, NJ: Paulist Press, p. 50.

4 R. S. Thomas, 2004, *Selected Poems*, London: Penguin Books, p. 91.

5 Marian Barnes, Mary Davies and David Prior, 2022, *Living Life in Common: Stories from the Pilsdon Community*, Market Harborough: Troubador.

6 Jalaluddin Rumi, 2004, *Rumi: Selected Poems*, Coleman Barks (trans.), London: Penguin Books, p. 104.

7 Day, *Selected Writings*, p. 278.

8 Emma Beddington, 2025, 'It's time to embrace Dugnadsånd – the Norwegian concept we all need right now', *The Guardian*, 23 March, https://www.theguardian.com/commentisfree/2025/mar/23/its-time-to-embrace-dugnadsand-the-norwegian-concept-we-all-need-right-now, accessed 19.01.2026.

9 Thomas Merton, 1998, *Dancing in the Waters of Life*, San Francisco, CA: Harper, p. 240.

7

Work

I'm in the barn at Rylands Farm sorting through bundles of damp willow, sharpening some thicker ones, which will be sides, and bunching thinner ones together for base and side weavers. It's a cool, damp autumn morning – perfect for basket-making as the withies won't dry out too quickly. I'm here at the invitation of the inspirational Julie Plumley, a former adult social worker, who after 20 years of seldom seeing any change in the clients she worked with, resigned and bought a farm, deciding to put her energy into working with young people excluded from or struggling at school. Growing up on a farm she knew the healing power of nature and the health-giving gift of physical work and reckoned that to offer this to young people alongside loads of positive mentoring she might be able to turn some lives around. Fifteen years on the results are remarkable, but I'm not here for the youngsters, I've been asked to run a basket-making session for the 'Countrymen's Club'.

Slowly, elderly men shamble in and take seats on straw bales in the barn, some guided in by carers, others dropped off by wives grateful for some respite. A bunch of bird boxes made last week are shifted off a couple of bales to make room for the dozen or so former farmers and agricultural workers. Some pull on wellies and get to work shaking straw in the cows' quarters, gently patting steamy bovine bodies in the soft October light. Others go over and scratch the back of the Kunekune pigs, another bottle feeds the orphan kid goats. The session begins with tea, and then I set to work building a base, splitting and splaying six rods to make the spokes of a wheel, and begin weaving around them. I talk as I work, telling them the difference between tips and butts at the end of each withie (I say 'tits' and 'bums' to see if they're listening and there's some raucous laughter). I ask if anyone has done weaving before. Ron tells me he's made corn dollies out of straw, but his hands are swollen with arthritis so he's not sure he'll be able to do it. I shove in the side stakes and bend them up to form the sides and look and look again at a man opposite; he looks familiar, but I wait to see if through conversation I can work out our connection. Once I've begun building the sides, weaving in and out, I pass it on to Ron, who immediately gets the hang of it and is delighted that he can do it. Conversation continues as I build the next base and sides and I pass the basket on. Then another and a thicket of willow stakes is formed, people spread out to avoid poking each other in the eye. One or two of the men struggle on their own so we do a few strands together, and in the end everyone's had a go.

I'm helping the man I thought I knew, who tells me in slurred speech he's called Andy. I have to hold the basket for him as, due to Parkinson's, he's only got one functioning arm. As his good hand deftly weaves, recognition comes as I remember that same hand pulling out a calf we were having trouble delivering when I was at Pilsdon ten years before. We'd sent for Andy Pollard the dairyman at the industrial farm next door. I was amazed how with one good arm and plenty of skill and experience he managed to get the young animal out that two of us had failed to deliver. Soon after that calving, he'd lost his job, then taken a job driving a small van delivering agricultural products to Dorset farms, which he'd loved. Sadly, due to his Parkinson's, he'd lost that job and, stuck at home, became very depressed, sometimes feeling suicidal. What had saved him was the Countrymen's Club: twice a week he found he wanted to get up to come to Rylands Farm where he could meet other retired farmers and have purpose. His wife also benefited from the break and the chance to meet other carers.

Countrymen's Club was dreamed up by Julie after her work with young people had been going a few years, when she saw her father, a retired farmer, also struggling with Parkinson's, getting depressed and worrying her mother. So, she applied the same principles of her work with young people to the older generation, using the restorative properties of nature, the daily and yearly rhythms of life on a farm, practical work and a welcoming environment. Julie told me 'some of the men who are now in care homes aren't allowed to go out if it's cold or raining. Imagine that – if you've spent all your life outside in all weathers, never feeling the rain on your cheeks – it's inhumane.'

Today the barn is not terribly warm, but the welcome is. I finish off the baskets, laying down the vertical stakes and weaving a border on each. The biggest basket we keep for the Harvest Festival next week; the other baskets people take home with a great sense of satisfaction. I tell the men I always feel better for having made a basket, in fact I always feel better when I'm working with my hands.

Recovering the joy of physical work

So many people now, like those elderly farmers, don't get to do much physical work or make things. Much of the UK economy is based around buying and selling. We truly have, in Napoleon's words, become a 'nation of shopkeepers'. In September 2025, The House of Commons Library showed that 83 per cent of people were employed in the service industries.[1]

Sharing physical activity together builds community but too often such work has been contracted out to machines or people working in other countries. I don't want to romanticize hard, backbreaking work that so many still do in our world, but I know there's an honesty and a connection that's built by grafting together that can never be duplicated in an office environment. Rather than make things ourselves, it's often cheaper and certainly quicker to buy something mass-produced. William Morris, who famously declared, 'Have nothing in your home that you do not know to be useful or believe to be beautiful',[2] would despair at so many ugly, cheap plastic goods. At Hilfield, rather than buy a cheap prefabricated shed, we'll instead build something solid and good looking, from timber we've milled ourselves or been gifted by a neighbour. In the building of a shed we'll learn new skills, form new friendships and the building itself will have a story that connects us to the place and each other. The temptation for me to build something on my own can sometimes be strong, as I don't have to negotiate with others, wait for them to turn up, help them, correct mistakes and often slow things down. Involving other people may take longer but, I'm learning, makes for a better and more creative building which belongs more truly to the community.

Hilfield has a large fourteenth-century bell donated from a redundant church in Wiltshire, which hangs on a wooden cradle near the entrance to the friary. It's sounded four times a day as a ten-minute warning before prayers and it's loud enough to be heard several fields away. Over the years the cradle began to rot, and I asked Philip Chatfield, a stone sculptor and former ship's carpenter, if he'd help me replace some of the timbers next time he came to stay. Philip's a burly looking man, built like a rugby prop forward, which indeed he was, with thick forearms muscled through 40 years of chipping stone. He survived the shipwreck of the *Maria Assumpta* off the Cornish coast in 1995 in which three people died by having the presence of mind to take off his lifejacket and dive under the waves as they hit the rocky coastline. This near brush with death and his artist's eye has given him a deep love for life and he's a joy to work with. As we worked on the bell frame he kept stopping me after each stage, encouraging me not to rush ahead but work steadily. First, we jacked up one side and with several belts of a hammer he smashed out the rotting timber. Then out came his wooden and brass angle finder and we marked up the notches in the new oak sleepers, which I roughly cut out with the chain saw. Then he smashed out the remaining dense oak with hammer and chisel. We stopped, drank some tea, then slid the big timbers into place and drilled holes through them into a concrete base, then pounded metal rods to secure them into the ground. Then another break and onto the other side, pausing for more tea. We worked quietly with the occasional comment from Philip, 'That'll do' and 'I'll buy that.' Slowly over a couple of days the frame was restored. Then we stained it and finally Philip cut out the words 'I will sing of your strength' into a horizontal beam and added gold leaf for a final garnish. Then we stood and looked at it, and I told Philip how I'd learnt from him not to rush, to work steadily, step by step and keep looking and being absorbed in the task. Philip speaks about living in the flow of things. He doesn't have a home but simply lives where he works, just like the stone masons of old. The tools he uses are the same as a medieval mason. Before he leaves us, he gives me a wood carving in relief of the Lamb of God with the Latin '*Dona Nobis Pacem*' (Give Us Peace) for the new shepherd's hut Ellie, Phil and I had built.

Working with him reminded me of working with Brother Mikael from Bose who told me, 'Jonathan, you work like a monk.' At first I thought he meant I worked hard, but later I discovered it was because I worked silently. As Thomas Merton wrote, 'And the deepest level of communication is not communicating but communion. It is wordless. Beyond words, and it is beyond speech and it is beyond concept, not that we discover a new unity but an older unity.'[3] Working with Philip affirmed this for me and certainly brought me peace.

Cistercian spirituality and manual work

Founded in the eleventh century, the Cistercian order of monks grew out of a desire to return to the radical simplicity they saw in the Rule of Benedict, which they felt had been watered down. It was felt that Benedict's saying, 'then are they only real monks if they live by the work of their hands, like our fathers the apostles',[4] had been lost as monastic houses expanded and contracted work out to lay people. The story is told of a Benedictine monk travelling to Clairvaux, the mother house of the Cistercians, and being amazed at how many well-educated men were involved with the getting in of the harvest. Guerric of Igny said, 'Work is a load by which, as ships are given weight, so hearts are given quiet and gravity, and in it the outward person finds a firm foundation and a settled condition.'[5]

Working with our hands can give us a sense of peace and dignity, and express equality and corporate solidarity. The Cistercian way is a far cry from the now-popular practice of working from home and conducting business by Zoom or Teams meetings where people don't physically meet. Such meetings feel much more businesslike and efficient but leave out the relational bits of shaking hands, making tea for someone, sharing food together, finding out how somebody's family is. The move towards conducting business remotely is dangerously taking us further away from the joy of human encounter. It's possible to go into a supermarket and use a self-checkout without speaking to another human being, and it is even more isolating to order something online. It's a long way from shopping at a traditional market, where you get the shout of the vendor, a smile, a bit of chat, a story about where the food came from, the handing over of coins and the return of change, and the meeting of neighbours.

In the film *Of Gods and Men*, which tells the story of seven Cistercian monks martyred at their Algerian monastery in 1995, we often hear the sounds of work before the camera reveals someone mixing cement or kneading bread. Seeing the monks at work individually and together helps the viewer partially enter their community life and grow in sympathy with the rugged beauty of their life in the Atlas Mountains. That they work in silence seems to add to the importance of their common tasks, allowing the camera to focus on their hands and show the joy of living in the moment. The simplicity of their life in turn makes it easier for them to befriend their Muslim neighbours in the impoverished village nearby.

Manual work can be healing

As the Cistercians know, working with our hands can be healing; many who come to live at or visit Hilfield experience the restorative power of spending an afternoon in the vegetable garden, weeding a newly planted hedge or chopping wood. I'm fortunate to live in the economy of Hilfield, where there are endless possibilities for hand work, and I notice how quickly I become stressed or grumpy when I spend too long in meetings, doing administrative tasks or sitting in a car. My body tells me that I'm missing something.

Writing about trauma in *The Body Keeps the Score*, Bessel van der Kolk says that for many who have experienced trauma the talking cure doesn't work. He says constantly reliving trauma with an unskilled therapist retraumatizes and adds power to the original trauma. His interaction and studies with survivors has led him to believe that healing and the control of the impulses that trigger fear are best accomplished through becoming aware of our bodies and being in touch with the body's reactions:

> Simply noticing what you feel fosters emotional regulation, and it helps you stop trying to ignore what's going on inside you. As I often tell my students, the two most important phrases in therapy and yoga are 'Notice that' and 'What happens next?' Once you start approaching your body with curiosity rather than fear everything shifts.[6]

Many of the guests at Hilfield in the early 1920s were men suffering from post-traumatic stress disorder, and the quiet rural setting, a disciplined life, and, above all, purposeful work aided the recovery of many. The community is looking to once again work with people from the army suffering with combat stress. A former general advising us said, 'It's all very well having a beautiful place for people to stay and lots of psychological support, but most of all these veterans need something to do.'

Working with the land

Hilfield offers a rich variety of manual labour. There's a varied economy of tasks, washing up, cleaning, cooking, bread-making, gardening, land management, animal husbandry, chopping wood, digging trenches, construction work, painting and decorating and many more physical challenges.

At Pilsdon, the tasks most sought after would be working with the animals, and people became quickly devoted to the chickens, the cows, the donkeys and particularly the pigs. The people we asked to look after the pigs were often people living with severe trauma, but seemed to stay longer than anyone else and never asked to change jobs. There was something about the pig's ability to communicate with people who'd lost trust in human beings that provided great solace. Brother Malcom at Hilfield seems to understand this special porcine and human affinity, and sometimes goes down to talk with the Hilfield pigs but often just stands silently with them after he's fed them. Malcom's friendship with the pigs feels totally mutual, each benefiting from the relationship.

Working the friary land often requires numbers and in the winter every Tuesday or 'Poosday' afternoon will find several people scraping the cows' winter quarters of muck and then shovelling it into our dung store where it will be transformed into garden manure. Perfect conditions for this weekly event are a bit of rain. Too dry and the shit sticks to the yard, too wet and the slurry slides off the spade. It's a great way to warm up on a cold winter's afternoon and a fine expression of our common life.

In contrast, the Hilfield hay harvest comes on the hottest days of the year. The tractor cuts the hay, but like medieval Cistercians large numbers of us go out to turn the hay to help it dry over a few days. It feels like a timeless scene looking over the rows of drying grass, picking out the contours of the field, noticing the hills around us, and then zooming in to the drying seedheads of yellow rattle, knapweed and various orchids and grasses. Working with the land does engender a real sense of belonging and kinship to it as we labour alongside it. Once the hay is dry the bailing begins and as the machine spits out rectangular blocks of compressed grass, we follow it, load them onto a trailer and stack them in the barn. It's hot, dusty and itchy work yet goes quickly as we chain the bales from person to person filling up the barn. Once all is safely stowed for the year we gather on bales in the barn and glasses of cider from the previous autumn apple harvest are raised celebrating our common endeavour.

Cider-making, like yogurt-knitting and bread from a sourdough are processes I love to be part of. For each, you simply start it off and let nature do the rest. For cider there's gathering fallen apples, chopping them, then squeezing them in our home-made juicer fashioned out of an old book press. Nothing is added, the juice is simply left a few weeks to ferment, then bottled. Likewise with the yogurt, milk is boiled, cooled to body temperature, a little live yogurt is added and the bacteria start multiplying, and 12 hours later runny milk has been transformed into a thick, creamy mass. There's a similar alchemy when the sourdough starter is added to flour and water and 24 hours later the dough is ready to go in the oven. Waiting allows delicious flavours to develop. Carlo Petrini, who started the 'Slow Food' movement in Italy after discovering that McDonald's had opened a restaurant on the Spanish Steps in Rome, would surely approve. Homemade food always has a story that connects us with the landscape and each other, and eating together is the seal on this very physical belonging to place and each other.

There's something about the waiting for the yogurt to form, the cider to brew, the bread to prove, that takes the process out of our hands and reminds us we're not in control but dependent on the work of micro-organisms, bacteria and chemistry. Good communities don't force people to be good or work hard but attract people into this process of growing together. 'The kingdom of heaven is like yeast that a woman took and mixed in with three measures of flour until all of it was leavened,' says Jesus in Matthew's Gospel (13.33). What Philip would describe as being in the flow.

Time and again at Pilsdon I saw something magical happen to people when they began to engage with animals, woodland and the vegetable garden. Hands-on engagement was transformative. Writing to Rosemary Radford Ruether, an urban theologian who in a previous letter has told him as a monk he was cut off from the world, Thomas Merton robustly responds,

> Tree planting and reforestation are not simply sentimental gestures in a region that has been ravaged by the coal and lumber companies ... You talk about God's good creation of the body, and all that, but I wonder if you have any realization at all of the fact that by working on the land a person is deeply and sensually involved with matter ... And for all their gnosticism, monks (at least in the West, where manual work has been held in honor) have had this sensual contact with matter.[7]

Our interaction with the landscape and the built environment, whether it's pruning trees or repairing a wall, help us belong further to the place or building that holds the community of people.

Working together with purpose

Work can help people find their place in community; it's good to be assigned a role and feel responsible for an aspect of community life, to be able to contribute to the common good and for others to see you doing it. Ruth Thurgar, the daughter of Percy Smith (who founded Pilsdon), writes,

> He was quite a slave driver in some ways. Sometimes he gave people tiny little jobs, because he knew they were either too old or weak or recovering from something, so it was something quite small. But they still got given a job, whatever it was, even if it was only polishing that brass pot, to give them all a meaning, to help with the running of the place, in a way to be seen as part of it.[8]

Still today at Pilsdon daily chores are assigned and every morning people set to work washing up, hoovering, laying tables, arranging flowers, folding tea towels, laying a fire, feeding the chickens, cleaning out the pigs. Once these individual jobs are completed, work with others begins in the garden, in the farmyard or on the buildings.

At Hilfield, big annual and one-off events bring people together in sometimes days of preparation. For our summer camps, hay has to be taken off the camping field, chairs and tables taken out of storage, the camp kitchen set up and a 200-seater canvas marquee is erected. Three 20-foot tent poles are carried across, along with 100 smaller poles and 100 three-foot metal tent pegs. It takes at least six people under the gentle direction of Brother Hugh to raise the large tent poles and tie them down with long guy ropes. Then the canvases are hauled like sails up on horizontal beams. They're laced together to form a single covering. Then the ring of metal on metal is heard as metal rods are hammered in for guy ropes for the side poles, then the poles are inserted into the edge of the tent and ropes secure them and tighten the canvas.

As well as providing a great communal space, the big marquee seems to symbolize our vision of community life as a big, safe, inclusive place where people can feel they belong. When the campers arrive, a meal is cooked by the community for 100 people. Later in the week we collect fallen branches and offcuts of timber for the campfire. So much of the life of the community seems to centre around washing and cleaning and carrying things from one place to another. Having an event or a big communal task broken into many smaller tasks seems to be a practical and visible expression of our life together.

Colin Macleod, sometimes referred to as 'The Birdman of Pollok' due to his spending nine days in a birch tree in 1997 to protest the building of the M77 through one of the few green spaces of the Pollok Estate in Glasgow, knew the value of creative work to help people recover from addiction. Following the road protests, which had galvanized the local community on an estate riddled by addiction, crime and gangs, he set up the GalGael trust based in Govan. The charity, through promoting the building, maintenance and sailing of traditional wooden Scottish boats, gives people wishing to recover from addiction a sense of purpose and a chance to become rooted in their heritage.

> We quickly realised that we could achieve many of our social and cultural aims by involving the community in building boats. For us boats are a metaphor for transformation – as we journey from one place to another – and tools for achieving our purpose.[9]

In the BBC Scotland film *The Birdman of Pollok*, the story is told of how a powerful vision of community built around traditional manual tasks of building and sailing timber boats led to the transformation of many lives. The film ends with the coffin of Colin Macleod being rowed by a crew of people in recovery in a birlinn – an ancient Hebridean galley – from the Isle of Mull for burial on Iona, a powerful symbol of how his vision had bound people together through engagement with culture, physicality and the natural world.

Playing together

When I lived on what the local press called 'the troubled Beechdale Estate', a large, much neglected, post-war council estate, we set up a whole series of locally inspired cultural activities alongside local residents and the inspirational Walsall Community Arts Team. We had a week-long arts festival of activities in schools, the pub, senior citizens club, the church, an exhibition of people's art and craft work, culminating in a carnival procession. Over the years we made banners and mosaics, started a gospel choir, had variety shows, exhibited local talent, put on community plays and pantomimes. The thing I enjoyed most was the Friday night seven-a-side football games we started. Each team had to include somebody under ten, somebody over 40 and be of mixed genders. The games were good for fitness, competitive, but never aggressive and always full of laughter.

Too often now sport and the arts are something we watch from a distance. We look at them on a screen, maybe go to a gallery, a cinema or a stadium if we can afford it. Increasingly life is performed for us, the observer. Undoubtedly, it's a powerful experience to be caught up in the drama of watching an exciting game with others, but I think it's even more binding to be playing the game or creating the art ourselves.

At Pilsdon we joined a local cricket competition, where we'd play several short games in the long summer evenings. Each year as the days lengthened we'd start practising on the one bit of flat land behind the barn. When new people joined us, we'd ask if they'd ever played cricket, or if they'd be willing to learn. We recruited neighbours and anyone who looked reasonably fit. One year we had a Sri Lankan and a mystery spinner from south India playing for us. Quite a lot of our team had played football but not cricket. With great excitement and high hopes, we'd climb into the community minibus and make our way to the lovely small ground surrounded by green hills and farmland. We were always the best supported team and for a number of years Sheila was our cricket correspondent, writing up match reports and, in the best traditions of *Test Match Special*, including the sheep, the identities of the birds swooping around us and passing farm machinery in her detailed reports of the game. We were always the most popular team to play because we never won. A lot of time was spent looking for the ball in the surrounding fields as regular sixes were hit off our bowlers. We kept the umpires busy signalling a lot of wides and when we went in to bat the game quickened up with a flurry of people being given out. We were a ragtag team of all ages and abilities, sometimes you could hear the rattling of medication in the pocket as one of our players ran into bowl. One of our players who'd done a lot of boxing went in gladiatorial style in shorts and bare chested. He slogged a couple of huge sixes and when given out leg before wicket started arguing with the umpire. I had to quickly run on to explain the rules and persuade him to leave. We invested great hopes in players who'd been to public schools, but they seldom succeeded. In 15 years we only won two games, really only one, as we later discovered our first ever victory was a result of a scoring error! It always felt well worth the effort as it brought the community together – preparations before the game, a trip out to a beautiful ground often bathed in golden evening light and long shadows, and so much laughter during and after the game, and later, on winter evenings, recalling the games.

Hilfield never managed to muster a cricket team, but is very good at encouraging people into art and craft activities. Every month there's a craft day where guests and day visitors to the community can bring something to do or learn a new skill. The day often starts chatty; but slowly, as people become immersed in their work, silence and serenity descends. People knit, sew, make straw hats, write icons, do wood cuts and when people do talk it's often to share important stuff. Sam Hale, a community arts worker who works a lot with marginalized women in the West Midlands, says when the hands are busy people feel able to talk. There's a settling and an opening up that comes with the often-forgotten art of creating something with our fingers, in a safe place and with others.

One year, leading up to Easter, we created a giant six-metre-high weaving, which we erected with scaffolding in the friary courtyard. People would climb up to weave plain cotton fabric and the occasional strip of red horizontally onto the loom. Once woven we lowered it and cut it out of the frame. For Palm Sunday we'd woven yucca leaves into it and rolled it out into the church for people to walk on as the procession entered the chapel. For Good Friday and Holy Saturday it was rolled up into a ball to represent the body of Christ and for Easter it was suspended across the chapel beams as liberated grave clothes.

Big public art can bind communities together, like the pride people take in Antony Gormley's Angel of the North. The giant puppet of a Syrian refugee girl, Amal, which made its way from Greece in 2021, brought out hundreds and thousands onto the streets in Europe to express solidarity with so many who'd made journeys from dangerous places.

There's a joy in making things by hand, each object having a story – as so beautifully described by Neil MacGregor in his radio series *A History of the World in 100 Objects*.[10] AI can now generate high-quality images of almost anything, but they somehow lack soul. As the Cistercians have always known, the Lord does indeed bless the work of our hands. I've always been grateful for the time I spend doing manual tasks and it's to gratitude that we now turn.

Questions

1 St Paul valued the work of his hands (1 Thess. 4.11). Has Christianity become too cerebral?

2 Why have we as a society become so cut off from manual work?

3 What might a new economy that valued practical work look like?

4 Are there activities, groups or clubs you know of that bring people together through common tasks?

5 Do you ever get lost in the moment while performing a simple manual job?

Practical suggestions

1 Notice your body's reactions, particularly what causes tension.

2 Practise yoga.

3 Make time to cook using local ingredients.

4 Grow some vegetables; volunteer at a local food-growing co-op.

5 Join a local conservation group.

Notes

1 House of Commons Library, 2026, 'Service industries: Economic indicators', *UK Parliament*, https://commonslibrary.parliament.uk/, accessed 21.01.2026.

2 William Morris, 1880, 'Lecture on the Beauty of Life', https://www.eb-j.org/pdfViewer/articles/MzI2OA, accessed 21.01.2026.

3 Thomas Merton, 1975, *The Asian Journal of Thomas Merton*, New York: New Directions, p. 308.

4 Timothy Fry (trans.), 1982, *The Rule of St Benedict*, Collegeville, MN: Liturgical Press, p. 69.

5 Andre Louf, 1989, *The Cistercian Way*, Kalamazoo, MI: Cistercian Publications, p. 114.

6 Bessel van der Kolk, 2015, *The Body Keeps the Score*, London: Penguin, p. 327.

7 Thomas Merton, 1995, *At Home in the World: The Letters of Thomas Merton and Rosemary Radford Ruether*, New York: Orbis Books, p. 43.

8 Marian Barnes, Mary Davies and David Prior, 2022, *Living Life in Common*, Market Harborough: Troubador, p. 79.

9 GalGael, n.d., 'What GalGael means', *GalGael*, https://www.galgael.org/what-galgael-means, accessed 19.01.2026.

10 Neil MacGregor, 2010, 'A History of the World in 100 Objects', https://www.bbc.co.uk/programmes/b00nrtd2/episodes, accessed 21.01.2026.

8

Gratitude

It's early morning on 18 December 2021, another dry day, thank God, as we clear the temporary car park next to the log pile of brash and flatten out the ruts, clearing space for the cars of over 200 visitors. Down in the field below stands the Hilfield marquee, shining white in the sun with its long red poles and long blue guy ropes, resembling a circus tent, symbolizing the joy of this festival day. Under its canvas a couple of people are rubbing the dust off rows of 1950s metal chairs. Someone's arranging dried flowers and another is placing orders of service on the clean seats. The tractor and trailer pull up and deliver hay bales as extra seating along with folded tables. I walk down to the two hastily constructed composting toilets and add a bucketful of fragrant sawdust next to the oval holes cut out of thick plywood. In the kitchen dozens of onions and several bulbs of garlic are being chopped for a huge pan of vegetable chili, an easy dish for feeding high numbers; someone else is up to their elbows rubbing crumble mix into a bowl. Someone's driving to the station to pick up Brother Sam. There's an air of excitement and joyful anticipation as we prepare for the 100th anniversary of the day three Franciscan Brothers walked the three miles from Evershot Station to begin community life at Hilfield.

An hour later visitors begin to pull into the car park and a team of green high-viz marshals welcome them and direct them to the marquee. Those who can't walk so well get on a wooden trailer and the tractor trundles them down the hill. Soon I catch strains of the first hymn, 'All Creatures of our God and King ...' and look out over the landscape, which has probably changed little over the last century, and I'm filled with a great sense of gratitude for this place and the gentle Franciscan presence here.

The service ends and the tractor delivers four large steaming pans of chilli and rice; tables are unfolded as the chapel becomes a dining area. Then it's time for planting. Richard, who manages the land, has suggested we plant 100 oaks, to give thanks for 100 years of Hilfield and the hope is that in 100 years' time the oaks will be providing shade to pasture in a much hotter ecosystem. We've asked 100 different people to bring a spade and plant an oak. Guests of honour include former Wayfarers, local ecologists, Gypsies and Travellers, members of Insulate Britain, neighbouring farmers, parish councillors, the High Sherriff, a bishop, the MP. Within an hour, 80-plus trees are planted and recorded. Then the Weymouth and Dorchester Extinction Rebellion samba band lead a procession over the fields back into the friary courtyard, where a blazing fire lights up the darkening day. Around the edge of the courtyard is a Swiss–German Christmas Market giving away cakes, biscuits, glühwein, coffee schnapps and non-plastic wooden cleaning utensils, all for a small donation. Then there's time for stories around the fire as former Brothers, past community members and guests share often hilarious tales of times at Hilfield, and express thanks for what the community has meant for them. The celebration ends with the big bell summoning people to Evening Prayer.

Celebrating life

In a way, this celebration was a magnified version of how the Hilfield Community seeks to live out each day. Daily giving thanks for the abundance of creation and our life together and seeking to include as wide a variety of people as possible in our life together. Gratitude is foundational for any person or community that wants to thrive. As a daily practice it's an antidote to individual despair, and corporate celebrations help bind communities together. Thanksgiving at the beginning of the day, and thankfulness throughout the day and at its ending, bring joy and contentment to community life. Meister Eckhart reflected, 'If the only prayer you say in your life is thank you, that is enough.' Pilsdon's founder Percy Smith said the two most important words in community life were 'thank you' and 'sorry'. Words that are too often missing from the entitled lives so many people live in Western society. Too many people focus on reaching out to what's next, and ironically the comparative luxury people have lived in since the 1960s, and our growing separation from the natural world that sustains us, has led to a less grateful society. Combine this with the doctrine of self-reliance coming from hyper-individualism and the thought you can buy everything you need rather than depending on your neighbours for help, and society is diminished. Robin Wall Kimmerer suggests in contrast that

> the relationships nurtured by gift thinking diminish our sense of scarcity and want. In that climate of sufficiency, our hunger for more abates and we take only what we need, in respect for the generosity of the giver. Climate catastrophe and bio-diversity loss are the consequences of unrestrained taking by humans. Might cultivation of gratitude be part of the solution?[1]

Communities don't work without gratitude and when moaning and recrimination become the norm, community comes under threat. That's why we need focuses for thanksgiving. A grace before meals reminds us where our food comes from and that all is gift. Tobias Jones, who started Windsor Hill Wood community, would, instead of a formal grace, ask each person gathered at the table what they wanted to give thanks for. It could be anything from delicious dumplings, a friend visiting, to thanks for another day of sobriety. At Hilfield we always celebrate people's birthdays with a card and individually themed cake, which allows us to remember them with gratitude. At Pilsdon whenever somebody gave us notice of leaving we'd present them with a framed postcard, tell a short story about them and thank them for their contribution to community life. Gratitude doesn't work if it's formulaic. It has to come from the heart.

Gratitude for the earth

Harvest festivals are a way of giving thanks for the land and all who work on it and a reminder that we are part of a bigger story. Last Harvest, I was at a celebration held at the Countrymen's Club. We sat on straw bales, sang a hymn, sang Louis Armstrong's 'What a Wonderful World', I said a few words of thanks, but the highlight for me was a reading of Dorset poet William Barnes' 'A Zong ov Harvest Hwome', where we all joined in lustily with the refrain at the end of each verse:

> The happy zight, the merry night,
> the Men's delight, the Harvest Hwome![2]

Then tea and scones dripping with home-made jam were served.

By weight at Hilfield our biggest harvest is water from a borehole filtered through chalk, followed by the hay crop. But what always feels most abundant is the apple crop. Cookers, eaters and crab apples over several weeks are processed by numerous people into puree to go with breakfast porridge, jams, juice, cider and vinegar. They come by the bucketload and their abundance always reminds me of Brother Sam's saying, 'To live in community you need bucketloads of generosity.' If we can have gratitude for the gifts of nature what naturally follows is thanksgiving for each other.

Looking at the natural world and looking again with a contemplative eye helps us live more gratefully. As Sanghasia, a Triratna Buddhist preceptor, has taught me, reverence is the basis for gratitude. Gratitude comes from appreciation and appreciation from awareness.

Joanna Macy, a Buddhist contemplative, deep ecologist and workshop leader in what she describes as the 'Work that Reconnects', begins with gratitude as the starting point in helping us reconnect with nature and face the challenges of the climate emergency and the ongoing destruction of natural systems. She says gratitude for the gift of life underpins all religious traditions and is the grounding of mysticism and art, and is vital in building community: 'Trust and gratitude feed each other: to deepen our capacity for thankfulness in difficult times, we need to learn from those who have mastered this quality.'[3]

Joanna Macy's model to bring about personal transformation and heal our disconnection from nature begins with gratitude, moves to lamentation – what she calls 'honouring our pain' – then to 'seeing anew' and finally 'going forth'. Her process is similar to the spirituality taught by Ignatius of Loyola, who also begins with gratitude. Ignatius would describe honouring our pain as realizing sin and its effect on us and the world; seeing anew for him would be entering into the life of Christ, and 'going forth' would be living the resurrection life.

Ignatius of Loyola and gratitude

Ignatius of Loyola was a Basque nobleman whose dream of military adventures and honour ended at the siege of Pamplona where he was seriously injured in both knees. His lengthy convalescence led to a conversion which continued in a cave near Manresa in the mountains of Montserrat. Here he wrote his *Spiritual Exercises*, which he offered for 'Christians and Pagans alike'. The Exercises are a series of scriptural and Christ-centred meditations, which, when shared with an experienced guide, enable the retreatant to get in touch with their inner life, noticing both creative and destructive forces. By choosing to follow the creative forces, the pilgrim on the inner journey finds their way to God and a sense of inner freedom. The Exercises are a manual to discern joy.

> Ignatius' Exercises begin with gratitude. His First Principle and Foundation asserts: All things in this world are also created because of God's love, and they become a context of gifts, presented to us so that we can know God more easily and make a return of love more readily.[4]

God's generosity underpins the purpose of the Exercises. Resting in God's goodness gives us the strength and confidence to explore some of the darker areas of ourselves and the world we live in. Poet and Jesuit Gerard Manley Hopkins captures this sense of gratitude throughout his writing, asking in his poem 'Spring': 'What is all this juice and joy'[5] and again in 'God's Grandeur' reminding us: 'The world is charged with the grandeur of God', but perhaps most forcefully in the poem 'That Nature is a Heraclitean Fire and the Comfort of the Resurrection', that at the heart of everything is an indestructible love:

> In a flash, at a trumpet crash
> I am all at once what Christ is, since he was what I am, and
> This Jack, joke, poor potsherd, patch, matchwood, immortal
> diamond
> Is immortal diamond.[6]

To keep returning to a sense of gratitude, the Exercises encourage the retreatant to do the Examen – a way of reviewing each day with gratitude. It's part of my daily practice. Towards the end of each day, I set aside ten minutes to review the day. Always starting with what has given me life, always resisting the temptation to go for what has been difficult and caused me anxiety. I will examine what has been difficult in the past day and notice these feelings, but only after I've immersed myself first in gratitude. As communities we will be better able to confront the challenges of a world of multiple overwhelmings if we are soaked in gratitude. Too often as individuals and communities our first responses come from what we perceive as threat. I wonder if as hunter-gatherers, humans were hard-wired to deal with threat, fear and danger first, to ensure survival. Ignatius urges us to begin with gratitude. I find reflecting prayerfully over the past day can compound my sense of gratitude. Experiencing again the joy evoked by light shining on autumnal beech leaves, the smell of a fresh-cut log, a child's smile, a precious conversation, can sometimes feel more powerful than the original experience.

Gerard Hughes writes,

> If we make a habit of reviewing the day in this way, we shall find that it will affect the way in which we see the world and everything and everyone in it. Life is God's gift to us. God is

> in the gift. Through this gift we are being called into the life of God. The extraordinary is in the ordinary, the ordinary in the extraordinary. Every bush is burning if only we have the eyes to see.[7]

Journalling our day, through writing, drawing it or even looking at photos on a phone is another way of compounding the life-giving experiences of the day or week.

Near the end of the Exercises, Ignatius introduces the 'Contemplation on the Love of God', another way of reinforcing a sense of gratitude by remembering that all is gift and to be shared. Love is not something to be hung on to but as it is freely given to us it needs to be shared out. Ignatius describes God's love as both a light shining down on us, and also a fountain lavishly pouring outwards. The Exercises conclude with the prayer 'Take and Receive':

> Take, Lord, and receive all my liberty, my memory, my understanding and my entire will – all that I have and call my own. You have given it all to me. To you Lord I return it; do with it what you will. Give me only your love and grace. That is enough for me.[8]

For community life, living from a place of gratitude for what we have received and not clinging to it, in the knowledge that what we give away will be returned again and again, is a remarkable gift because it creates a non-possessive culture of sharing. The realization that what we have is pure gift allows us to share what we have with each other and live in real freedom together. It's a powerful rebuttal to the narratives of scarcity and private individual security, and hanging on to our hard-earned property. If all we have is gift then we need not protect it, but rather we can gift it to others.

Living in gratitude

I'm often touched by the gratitude shown by some of the elderly and frail friars at Hilfield who seem so frequently to be saying 'thank you' and saying it with such graciousness. When we finally fix a leaking toilet in the Brothers' house it's a thank you with a gentle smile, emanating from a life orientated towards gratitude. Such small gestures build community and make you want to live in the place. We try to run Hilfield as a 'Gift economy', which means nobody pays to stay here but our guests are invited to give a donation. This is incredibly freeing as though we do our best to keep the guest rooms clean and produce good home-cooked food, if we do forget to clean someone's room or burn the lunch no one's going to get sacked and our corporate image won't be damaged! Nobody gets paid for living and working here either. We are all volunteers receiving expenses, which means the running of the place depends entirely on people's willingness to give themselves to our life together. Some people inevitably have greater capacity for generosity, and they counterbalance those who are more grudging with their time and enthusiasm. As a community, we try and ensure we don't exploit people's generosity, making sure people have good time off and the time and encouragement to pursue their own interests. It's wonderful to see young people in particular grow in confidence and increase their willingness to serve others. Just as I am mentored by the good grace of older Brothers so I hope I can encourage others. Often the influx of one or two enthusiastic and self-giving young volunteers can significantly lift the mood of the place and remind us of the gift of sharing life together. We have a culture where it's fine to make mistakes, and I'm still amazed at how little judgement there is here. If someone is struggling with a job there are always people ready to assist.

This living in gratitude challenges the prevailing myths of scarcity promoted by the far right and others to foster fear and hatred of immigrants, Gypsies and Travellers and others. 'They're stealing our jobs, taking our houses, putting extra strain on the NHS.' (The truth is that immigration brings a net benefit to the economy. Once single men gain asylum they regularly become homeless rather than taking up housing. Forty-five per cent of those working in the NHS are from minority ethnic groups.) The cutting of international aid to fund defence spending, announced by the Labour government in February 2025, is symptomatic of a growing selfishness and isolation from others which, far from bringing the nation greater security, will further destabilize the world.

What living in community continually teaches me is that there is always enough if we are willing to share it. Time and again I discover that if I'm prepared to be generous with my time and even when I'm tired give time to listen to someone or help with a job, things still manage to get done.

It's true that hatred can unite us for a while – witness the galvanizing effect of a country going to war. Polarizing narratives that scapegoat groups can be politically popular, as shown by the surge in support for far-right parties in Europe. Xenophobia, the fear of the stranger, is a powerful human emotion and plays on our human need for security, but its tendency is to divide and eventually will destroy those groups who pursue it. *Philoxenia*, the love of the stranger, though more complex and demanding, is something that builds up community.

At Hilfield, the community is diverse, ranging from a babe in arms to a 78-year-old. We are men, women, non-binary, trans, lesbian and gay, some committed to chastity, some in relationships. We have European, African, Latin American and Pacific Island people sharing life together. We have those who are theologically conservative, liberals, radicals, Buddhists, Quakers all trying to live well together. There are inevitable tensions but our common vision and commitment to living in the generous love of God motivates us to live generously together. Our guests come from a variety of backgrounds, some very wounded and opinionated, but with grace we try and model tolerance and acceptance and many come away changed by this. It's wonderful to see generosity breaking down fear and hatred.

Community solidarity

In November 2021, Hilary Bond and I travelled to the COP 26 meeting in Glasgow, not so much to protest but to pray for international agreements that might help slow and even reverse the human contribution to the climate crisis and the destruction of nature. The driver of the first bus we boarded on our arrival – in that most generous of cities – waved us on for free. Our host for the first night was a councillor for the Scottish Nationalist Party who was outraged at how hotels and hostels were hiking their prices for the conference and so offered free lodging for activists. He made us very welcome, saying, 'I've got nothing against the English, I just don't want to be ruled by them!'

Throughout the next few days we were warmly greeted by locals and activist comrades alike. On the last night, we met up with Brother Clark Berge, a Franciscan who invited us to dinner with the couple he was staying with in Pollokshields and two of their friends. At dinner we got talking about immigration and our host said, 'What Nicola Sturgeon our First Minister says is that if you come to live in Scotland that makes you Scottish.' How different, I thought, to the 'hostile environment' promoted by the very English Home Secretary Theresa May. I asked if they knew anything about the failed immigration removal of two asylum seekers in Pollokshields that had gone viral on social media. I'd remembered seeing hundreds of local people surrounding a Home Office van and the crowd chanting, 'Let them go, they're our neighbours.' Our hosts replied with great pride:

> Well, as it happens, this is Kenmure Street where it happened. What the immigration guys didn't know was that they parked their van outside the house of a local activist called Dexy. He immediately messaged all his mates and neighbours then slipped under the bus, wrapping himself around the front axle of the Border Security bus. On your way home you'll see a hot water bottle hanging on a lamppost. Someone brought that out to keep him warm.

'Oh and by the way,' they went on, 'we wrote a song about it called "Dexy's under the Bus". Would you like to hear it?'

I turned and grinned at Hilary and Clark, as the instruments came out and the song was played. As we walked back we passed the limp hot water bottle, a sign of the generosity of this community and a reminder that community solidarity is the antidote to fear and despair. I felt gratitude that night for our hosts, the meal, the music and the way a community had come together to support its neighbours.

Celebration binds communities

Community celebrations reflect gratitude and express it publicly, binding people together, be they religious festivals, weddings that last days or an open-top bus ride as the local football team displays its trophy around the town.

Billy Welch, proud Romany Gypsy, organizes the annual Appleby Horse Fair every June in the Cumbrian hills. It's remarkable to visit and see the town filled with Romany Gypsies celebrating their culture. As you pass a local pub you'll see horses tied up on railings outside, and see young women riding bareback on huge Gypsy Cobs on the High Street. In the river, with people watching from the stone-arched bridge, Travellers wash their horses in the shallows and then ride out to swim through deep water. Up on Fair Hill people cook over open fires to the backdrop of clouds hanging over the Cumbrian hills. As night falls people gather round to share stories that they know will keep their culture alive. Billy says, 'It's the one time of the year when my people can feel really free, Appleby is our Mecca.'

Living at the Franciscan friary of Hautambu in the Solomon Islands in the South Pacific, I was continually learning how people belong to one another and the natural world. 'Me, you and everyone' was a constant refrain, a little like the constant background sound of the surf hitting the coral reef. When I went out to work with the Brothers clearing scrub with a bush knife, planting casava, rebuilding a road washed away by flooding, no one was ever outwardly in charge, we just seemed to work as one. At the end of the working day, we'd go for a 'swim' and wash the sweat off in the sea. After evening prayer we'd walk up in the dark to the communal dining area, lit by a diesel generator which provided light for an hour. Supper ended with short prayers, people were thanked for their work and any announcements made. One evening I thought I heard them say in pidgin that the generator would come on at midnight. I dismissed this as fanciful due to my poor language skills. The lights did come on at midnight, the reason being that we had killed a pig earlier for the Feast of the Ascension and needed to cut it up by night when the flies were missing. My high-powered head torch was much appreciated as we first scorched the bristles off the pigskin then people began to butcher it. Alongside this, the 200 or so people gathered for the feast all contributed to a wide variety of tasks – lighting and tending the fire, and, once it began to glow, adding large round stones. Others wrapped meat and fish in small parcels with banana leaves. People grated cassava and coconut, then wrung out the coconut to produce juice. They then wrapped up the mixture with banana leaves in the shape of a large brie cheese in order to slow cook it, and produce Kustom pudding. Others weaved strands of coconut leaves to make individual pockets to boil rice in. Once the stones on the fire were glowing red, more banana leaves and hessian were put on top, the parcels of meat and fish added, then insulated with more leaves and soil on top, then 'me, you and everyone' all went to rest, apart from one Brother on sentry duty to keep the dogs away.

The next day, for the first time I really understood what a feast day in the church is, as we entered the tin-roofed chapel filled with incense and sang surging songs with natural harmonies, celebrated the Eucharist, and then went down to the beach for the food. We sat on the ground, either side of long green banana table mats and opened our brown parcels of meat and fish, pockets of rice, accompanied by chunks of orange pineapple, red watermelon and yellow cubes of Kustom pudding. Later on, we walked up the hill to the friary for some traditional dancing, accompanied by bamboo pan pipes struck with drumsticks whose ends were tied on pieces of flip flop recycled from the beach. Much laughter, much joy.

Celebration and rituals of thanksgiving serve to bind communities together, and they seem to persist most in places like the Solomon Islands where people have little material security, but perhaps because of this know their need of one another. Community celebrations remind us of our common vision and are visible signs of our belonging together.

At Pilsdon the biggest celebration of the year is 'The Anniversary', which is celebrated on the Sunday nearest 16 October (the day in 1958 that Percy bought Pilsdon Manor). In the days leading up to it people will begin baking, clearing the house and tidying up the garden and farmyard. The small medieval church is decorated with produce from the garden and the land, compost, buckets, shovels and pitch forks. If there are musicians, a band will practise. On the day, visitors park in a field, tea and home-made biscuits are served at 11am, the church is packed at 12pm then there are long queues for lunch. At 3pm it's time to meet the trustees for a report from the past year and a discussion of future plans, then tea and the ritual cutting of the anniversary cake. A couple of hundred people visit for the day, some for the first time, but for many it's about keeping their bond with the community going.

Religious festivals are a way of keeping and making public the faith and in turn reminding the devotees and members of the stories that make up the tradition and continue to inspire. Whether it be Hanukkah, Diwali, Eid or Christmas, the common theme is that we belong to the ummah, the sangha, the body of Christ. Community celebrations remind us that we are made to be together and that hardship and alienation can be overcome when we support one another. They are the antidote to a culture that preaches self-reliance, independence and individual choice. A culture that believes you can buy happiness and security and says that what is all important is meeting our own needs, doing things to benefit me. Hyper-individualism never really works. It leads to stress, fear of the other and perpetual anxiety. Christmas of course is the extreme example of this cultural neurosis. At Hilfield, not a Christmas carol is sung before Midnight Mass but instead the four weeks leading up are spent in the season of Advent. Advent is a time of waiting, pregnant with not knowing, sitting in the darkness longing for the light. There is also physical preparation for the feast: Christmas puddings are communally stirred; fruit cakes baked and left to mature. On Christmas Eve trees appear and are decorated, barrowfuls of greenery are gathered from the woodland and the chapel is filled with the scent of western red cedar leaf. After the first carols of Midnight Mass mulled home-brewed cider is served by a fire in the courtyard and it feels like the Light has come.

Gratitude leads to gratitude

Gratitude compounds itself; the more you have of it, the more you live intentionally with it, the more it grows. It's no surprise to me that the people who seem to embody this most are elderly – it's as though they've had a lifetime of practice. The world is also populated with bitter old men, and disastrously some major world leaders, particularly those who hang on to power for years, contribute to great amounts of violence and fear in the world. If they had only learned to live more generously then we'd have a more peaceful and sustainable planet. *The Book of Joy* is a record of the encounter between the remarkably gentle and smiley elderly Dalai Lama and Archbishop Desmond Tutu. The book is full of laughter and gentle teasing and a generous openness to each other's traditions. Reflecting on generosity, Tutu comments,

> The Dead Sea in the Middle East receives fresh water but it has no outlet, so it doesn't pass the water out. It receives beautiful water from the rivers, and the water goes dank. I mean it goes bad. That's why it's the Dead Sea. It receives and does not give. And we are made much that way too. I mean, we receive and must give. In the end generosity is the best way of becoming more and more joyful.[9]

Desmund Tutu often spoke of 'ubuntu' from his Xhosa language, which translates as 'a person becomes a person through other people', or 'I am because you are'. He continually stressed it, to show our dependence on one another and the natural world.

Looking at the world through the generous lens of community illustrates that we are all interconnected and that the narratives of separation and of them and us will lead us to stagnation and loneliness.

When our bellringer at Hilfield, Keith McDonald, became ill with inoperable cancer, it would have been a very stressful thing for Keith to have gone for treatment in hospital or even in a hospice, so he and the community decided to keep him at home. Fortunately, one of the Community was a nurse with lots of experience of end-of-life care. Keith was able to keep going and rang the bells up to the last two weeks of his life when he took to his bed. On the evening of his death, I joined Brother Malcom and Brother Hugh as we prayed for his soul and then he lay in state as the next morning various members of the community and some of the children visited his bedroom to say goodbye. Then his body was sent off for cold storage while we dug the grave in our burial ground and I wove a willow coffin. We then collected various famous and oft-repeated sayings of Keith, like 'I keep law and order round here', 'Let me be the Judge', 'I'm your Commanding Officer, you know', 'Carry on, Sergeant!', 'I'm your Emperor Nero, you know', or, as we turned down the precipitously steep hill on the final road to Hilfield, 'Fasten your seatbelts we're coming in to land.' A board with the quotes and various pictures from Keith's life was prepared. The day of his funeral, instead of the customary Bible and crucifix that are placed on a friar's coffin, a banana and *Radio Times* decorated its lid. He used to playfully shoot guests with a banana and liked to plan his TV watching a few days in advance. As his body was shouldered from the chapel to the cemetery, the bell tolled 83 times to mark the span he'd been allotted. As we prepared to lower him into the grave I couldn't help muttering 'Carry on, Sergeant' to those next to me gripping the burial straps. We filled in the grave communally, then made the short walk up the avenue of limes to the warmth of a blazing fire and the comfort of food and drink. We were full of gratitude for a man who had lived with us 67 years of the 100 years of the friary community, been held by it and been able to contribute faithfully and sometimes outrageously to it.

Like Hilfield, a life well lived.

Questions

1 Where do I find gratitude stressed in the Bible?

2 What corporate celebrations of gratitude that you have been part of really stand out?

3 How much do I live from a place of gratitude rather than fear?

4 What prevents people living more gratefully in our society?

5 Who are the people who inspire you with their generous living?

Practical suggestions

1 Cultivate gratitude and notice kindness.

2 Consider doing the Examen each evening: ignatianspirituality.com.

3 Take a sensory walk, noticing sights, sounds, smells, tastes and textures in the environment around you. Notice nature's abundance.

4 Think about how the Gift Economy might work in your life, and read *The Serviceberry* by Robin Wall Kimmerer.

5 Keep saying thank you.

Notes

1 Robin Wall Kimmerer, 2024, *The Serviceberry*, London: Penguin, p. 12.

2 William Barnes, 1984, *The Dorset Poet*, Wimborne: Dovecot Press, p. 100.

3 Joanna Macy and Chris Johnstone, 2012, *Active Hope*, Novato, CA: New World Library, p. 50.

4 David Fleming, 1996, *Draw Me into Your Friendship*, Chestnut Hill, MA: Institute for Jesuit Sources, p. 27.

5 Gerard Manley Hopkins, 1971, *Poems and Prose*, London: Penguin, p. 28.

6 Hopkins, *Poems and Prose*, pp. 65–6.

7 Gerard Hughes, 2004, *God in All Things*, London: John Murray Press, p. 58.

8 Fleming, *Draw Me into Your Friendship*, p. 81.

9 Douglas Abrams, 2016, *The Book of Joy*, London: Penguin, p. 264.

www.ingramcontent.com/pod-product-compliance
Lightning Source LLC
LaVergne TN
LVHW091326150826
845673LV00006B/1787

9781786227164